easy christmas cut-up cakes
FOR KIDS

easy christmas cut-up cakes
FOR KIDS

melissa barlow

GIBBS SMITH
TO ENRICH AND INSPIRE HUMANKIND
Salt Lake City | Charleston | Santa Fe | Santa Barbara

**For my mom, Nancy, who lifts
my spirits all year long**

First Edition
13 12 11 10 09   5 4 3 2

Text © 2009 Melissa Barlow
Photographs © 2009 Zac Williams

Published by
Gibbs Smith
P.O. Box 667
Layton, Utah 84041

1.800.835.4993 orders
www.gibbs-smith.com

Designed and produced by Dawn DeVries Sokol
Manufactured in Shenzhen, China in November 2009 by Toppan Printing Co. (SZ) Ltd.
Gibbs Smith books are printed on either recycled, 100% post-consumer waste, FSC-certified papers
or on paper produced from a 100% certified sustainable forest/controlled wood source.

Library of Congress Cataloging-in-Publication Data

Barlow, Melissa.
  Easy Christmas cut-up cakes for kids / Melissa Barlow. — 1st ed.
     p. cm.
  ISBN-13: 978-1-4236-0517-1
  ISBN-10: 1-4236-0517-9
  1. Cake. 2. Holiday cookery. I. Title.
  TX771.2.B37 2009
  641.5'68—dc22
                                        2008054222

contents

introduction

Now you can easily bake and decorate your very own shaped Christmas cake! This book is full of easy cake ideas that you can make for special occasions—especially Christmas. Choose your favorite pattern and surprise your family and friends with your creative genius!

READY, SET . . .

Before you start baking, please do two very important things:

    1. Ask permission from your parent or guardian.

    2. Find an adult helper to join you in the fun—mainly to keep you safe but also to answer questions you might have about the recipe or ingredients. In this book you will use electric mixers, hot ovens, and knives. You need an adult helper and must always be careful!

GO BAKE!

The first step when making any recipe in this book is to *read the whole recipe first.* Search the cupboards to make sure you have the right pans for the cake you've chosen. Then gather all the ingredients together so they will be handy.

    Now turn on the oven to the temperature noted in the recipe. Let the oven preheat (reach the desired temperature) while you grease the cake pans and mix the batter. An oven that has been preheated will cook the cake evenly. And pans that have been well greased will let the cake pop out in one piece after it has cooled a bit.

    After mixing the ingredients together and making a deliciously smooth batter, carefully transfer the batter to the greased pans. Then your adult helper can

help you carefully put the pans into the oven. Set a timer and then relax until it rings, dings, or whistles at you. To test for doneness, have your adult helper insert a toothpick in the center of the cake. If it comes out clean, the cake is done.

Let the cakes cool completely before you frost them. This will help keep crumbs out of your frosting. You can even bake the cake a day before you frost it.

LET'S FROST

Frosting is one of the most important parts of decorating your cake. Frosting can be messy, so be very careful as you decorate, and ask your adult helper to work with you.

To help keep *you* clean, wear an apron. To help keep *your cake plate* clean, stick little pieces of wax paper just under the edges of your cake. When you finish frosting the cake, just pull out the wax paper pieces and throw them away. Your cake plate won't have frosting all over it.

What Frosting Should I Use?

There are many yummy flavors of frosting that you can buy. Some of these are whipped, making them easier to spread. Sometimes you need frosting that is stiffer, such as for squeezing through a decorating bag to draw lines or make shapes. For stiffer frosting (or if you want to flavor it yourself), you and your adult helper can make these easy recipes instead of buying frosting from the store.

Vanilla Buttercream Frosting
1 stick margarine or butter, softened*
3 to 4 tablespoons water or milk
2 teaspoons vanilla*
Pinch salt (optional)
1 pound (about 4 cups) powdered sugar

Beat margarine or butter, water or milk, and vanilla together with an electric hand mixer until smooth. Add salt if using. Gradually beat in the powdered sugar 1 cup at a time. If the frosting is too thick, add more water or milk by the teaspoon until it reaches the right consistency. If it is too thin, add a little more powdered sugar.

*Substitute 1 cup regular vegetable shortening and clear vanilla if you want a whiter, less cream-colored frosting.

Chocolate Buttercream Frosting
1 stick margarine or butter, softened*
3 to 4 tablespoons water or milk
2 teaspoons vanilla
Pinch salt (optional)
$1/2$ cup cocoa powder
3 to 4 cups powdered sugar

Beat margarine or butter, water or milk, and vanilla together with an electric hand mixer until smooth. Add salt if using. Beat in cocoa powder. Gradually beat in the powdered sugar 1 cup at a time. If the frosting is too thick, add more water or milk by the teaspoon until it reaches the right consistency. If it is too thin, add a little more powdered sugar.

*Substitute 1 cup regular vegetable shortening if desired.

smiley snowman

1. Make cake mix according to package directions.
Put two-thirds of the batter into a greased 1.5-quart
bowl and the remaining batter in a greased 1-quart
bowl. Bake at 350 degrees F for 26 to 32 minutes
and then carefully remove the smaller bowl from
the oven. Bake larger cake another 5 to 10 minutes,
or until a toothpick inserted in the center comes out
clean. Cool cake in pans for 10 minutes, and then
invert and cool completely on a wire rack.

PANS: 1 (1.5-quart)
glass bowl
1 (1-quart) glass bowl

1 cake mix, any flavor

White frosting

Yogos Rollers or Fruit by the
Foot

Peanut M&Ms

1 tube black frosting

1 baby carrot

Black licorice

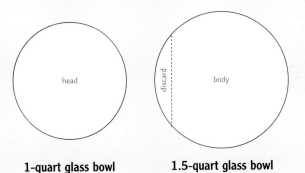

1-quart glass bowl   1.5-quart glass bowl

2. Cut the large cake according to the diagram.
Place the cakes on a large serving platter or foil-
wrapped board to create the snowman.

SERVES: 10 to 12

13

3. Frost the entire cake with white frosting. Make a scarf using Yogos Rollers or Fruit by the Foot.

4. Gently press the M&Ms into the snowman's belly for buttons, and cut small pieces of black licorice to make his smile.

5. Use the black frosting to draw the circles of the snowman's eyes and then stick a small piece of black licorice in each for the pupils. Finally, finish by sticking in his carrot nose and licorice arms.

Variation: You can use chocolate chips in place of the licorice for his mouth and eyes.

sweet angel

1. Make cake mix according to package directions. Divide batter equally between each pan. Bake at 350 degrees F for 27 to 32 minutes and then carefully remove from oven. Cool cake in pans for 10 minutes, and then invert and cool completely on a wire rack.

PANS: 1 (8-inch) round pan
      1 (8-inch) square pan

1 cake mix, any flavor

Pink or peach frosting

White frosting

Brown frosting

Red frosting

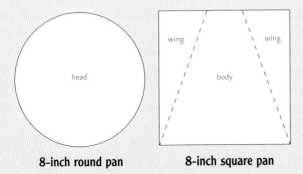

8-inch round pan   **8-inch square pan**

2. Cut the square cake according to the diagram. Place the cakes on a large serving platter or foil-wrapped board to create the angel and her wings.

3. Frost the round cake smoothly with the pink or peach frosting. Frost the angel's body and wings smoothly with the white frosting.

SERVES: 10 to 12

15

4. Using a decorator's bag with a round tip, give the angel curly hair by swirling the brown frosting on top of her head and then draw the eyes and eyelashes. Using red frosting, give the angel a little oval mouth.

5. Finally, using a decorator's bag with a star tip, give the angel a halo as shown in the picture and outline her body.

Variation: Sprinkle colorful sprinkles on the angel's wings!

peppermint candy

PANS: 1 (9-inch) round pan
1 (8-inch) square pan

1 cherry chip cake mix

White frosting

Red sprinkles

1 tube red frosting

1. Make cake mix according to package directions. Put 2½ cups batter in a greased 9-inch round pan and the remaining batter in a greased 8-inch square pan. Bake at 350 degrees F for 27 to 32 minutes and then carefully remove from oven. Cool cake in pans for 10 minutes, and then invert and cool completely on a wire rack.

2. Cut the square cake according to the diagram. Place the cakes on a large serving platter or foil-wrapped board.

9-inch round pan

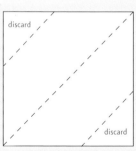

discard

discard

8-inch square pan

3. Frost the entire cake smoothly with white frosting. Using a piece of scratch paper, draw a 9-inch circle and cut it into "pie" pieces. Set the cutouts on top of the round cake; then remove every other one. Cover the parts of the frosting that are showing with a thick layer of red sprinkles. Press down gently with your fingers to

SERVES: 10 to 12

make sure the sprinkles stay in place, and then
remove the remaining pieces of paper.

4. Using the red tube frosting, outline the candy as
shown in the photo, the ends of the "wrapper"
jagged on each side as well.

Variation: Use a chocolate cake
mix and then crushed peppermint
candies instead of red sprinkles.

gingerbread man

PANS: 9 x 13-inch pan

1 chocolate cake mix

Chocolate frosting

White frosting

1 tube black or black gel
  frosting

M&Ms and gumdrops

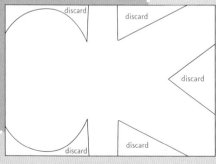

9 x 13-inch pan

SERVES: 10 to 12

1. Make cake mix according to package directions. Pour batter into pan. Bake at 350 degrees F for 27 to 32 minutes and then carefully remove from oven. Cool cake in pans for 10 minutes, and then invert and cool completely on a wire rack.

2. Cut the cake according to the diagram. Place the cake on a large serving platter or foil-wrapped board.

3. Frost the entire cake smoothly with the chocolate frosting.

4. Using a decorator's bag with a round or star tip, outline the entire gingerbread man and draw his face, using white frosting for the eyes and black or black gel frosting for the pupils. Make dots for his buttons, and make squiggles on his arms and legs.

5. Finish decorating by using M&Ms or gumdrops.

toy train

1. Mix cake mix according to package directions. Evenly pour batter into each mini loaf pan. Bake at 350 degrees for 20 to 23 minutes, or until done. Cool cakes in pans 10 minutes and then cool completely on a wire rack.

2. Cut one mini loaf cake in half as shown in the diagram. Position one of the halves on top of another mini loaf cake to make the engine. Throw away or eat the other half. Place the engine on a plate or foil-wrapped board, followed by the remaining mini loaf cakes.

discard

5 mini loaf pans

3. Frost the engine red and then draw the windows with the white tube frosting. Press two Oreos into the frosting on each side of the engine to make the wheels.

PANS: 5 mini loaf pans

1 cake mix, any flavor
Red frosting
Green frosting
1 tube white frosting
16 Oreos
1 plain ice cream cone
White cotton candy or mini
   marshmallows
Red and green M&Ms, and
   other Christmas candies

SERVES: 8 to 10

23

4. Frost the next car red, the next green, and the last one green. Press 2 Oreos into each side of the cars to make the wheels.

5. Frost the ice cream cone red and position on the front of the engine. (You may need to cut part of the cake away so it sits securely.) Place some cotton candy or mini marshmallows on top to look like smoke.

6. Stick M&Ms in the center of each Oreo wheel with a little frosting. Decorate the rest of the cars by loading them up with Christmas candies.

Variation: You can use black licorice to connect the cars!

o christmas tree

1. Make cake mix according to package directions. Pour batter into a 9 x 13-inch pan. Bake at 350 degrees F for 27 to 32 minutes and then carefully remove from oven. Cool cake in pan for 10 minutes, and then invert and cool completely on a wire rack.

2. Cut the cake according to the diagram. Position the two smaller triangle pieces together to create one large triangle, and frost the top light green. Place the big triangle on top and then frost the entire cake smoothly with light green frosting.

3. Cut the candy bar in half and stack the pieces together to make the tree's trunk. Press them gently into the frosting at the bottom of the tree.

4. Put some red frosting in a decorator's bag with a star tip and make a garland on the tree. Finish by decorating with Peanut M&Ms or other Christmas candies as desired.

PANS: 9 x 13-inch pan

1 chocolate cake mix

Light green frosting

King-Size Snickers or Milky Way bar

Red frosting

Red Peanut M&Ms

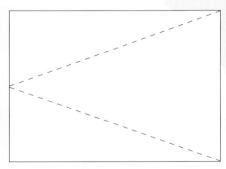

9 x 13-inch pan

SERVES: 10 to 12

toy drum

PANS: 2 (8-inch) round pans

1 cake mix, any flavor

White frosting

Light green frosting

Christmas-colored M&Ms

1 tube red frosting or red
   string licorice

2 pieces red licorice

2 Christmas Whoppers

1. Make cake mix according to package directions. Pour batter into pans. Bake at 350 degrees F for 27 to 32 minutes and then carefully remove from oven. Cool cake in pans for 10 minutes, and then invert and cool completely on a wire rack.

2. Using a knife or some thread, level the tops of each cake round; discard or eat the excess.

3. Place one cake cut side up on a large serving platter or foil-wrapped board and, using some of the white frosting, frost the top only. Once you have finished frosting the top, place the second cake cut side down over the frosting. (This will make it easier to frost because then you won't have to deal with the crumbs from cutting the cake level!)

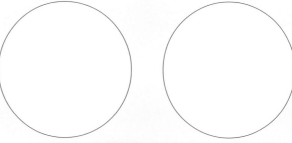

2 (8-inch) round pans

SERVES: 10 to 12

4. Frost the very top of the cake with white frosting, making sure to go all the way to the edge all around. Frost the sides of the cake with light green frosting so it touches the white from the top.

5. Place the M&Ms around the top and bottom of the cake, and then, using the red tube frosting, draw the lines around the sides of the drum as shown in the picture. Or, cut several pieces of red string licorice into equal lengths and use to create the zigzag lines.

6. Cut the tip of one end of each piece of licorice. Dab a little white frosting on the cut end and lay the licorice across the drum. Stick the Christmas Whoppers on the cut ends with the frosting.

santa's hat

PANS: Muffin pan
9 x 13-inch pan

1 cake mix, any flavor

Red frosting

White frosting

White miniature marshmallows

Red sprinkles

1. Make cake mix according to package directions. Spoon some batter into one cup of a lightly sprayed muffin pan, and then pour the remaining batter into the 9 x 13-inch pan. Bake at 350 degrees F for 17 to 20 minutes and then remove pan with cupcake. Bake cake 10 to 13 minutes more and then carefully remove from oven. Cool cake in pan for 10 minutes, and then invert and cool completely on a wire rack.

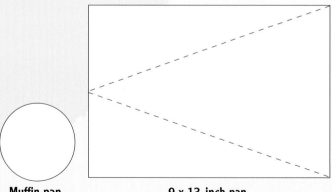

Muffin pan   **9 x 13-inch pan**

SERVES: 10 to 12

2. Cut the cake according to the diagram. On a serving platter, position the two smaller triangle pieces together to create one large triangle and then frost the top red. Place the big triangle on top and then use the red frosting to frost all but one strip of the triangle at the bottom. Frost the bottom strip white, as well as the top and sides of the cupcake.

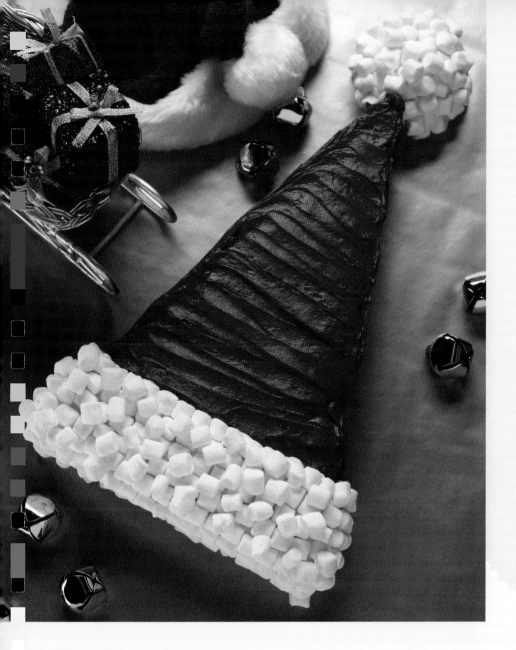

3. Completely cover the white frosting areas with the miniature marshmallows.

4. Lightly sprinkle the red-frosted area with the red sprinkles.

snowflake stocking

1. Make cake mix according to package directions. Pour batter into pan. Bake at 350 degrees F for 27 to 32 minutes. Carefully remove from the oven. Cool cake in pan for 10 minutes, and then invert and cool completely on a wire rack.

2. Cut the cake according to the diagram. On a serving plate, position the rectangle piece at the top of the stocking.

3. Frost the stocking smoothly with the light blue frosting and the rectangle part with the white frosting. Decorate the blue frosting with blue sprinkles, if desired.

4. Completely cover the white frosting with the miniature marshmallows.

5. Using a decorator's bag with a small round tip, draw on the snowflakes and then stick on the marshmallows as shown in the picture.

PAN: 9 x 13-inch pan

1 cake mix, any flavor

Light blue frosting

White frosting

Blue sprinkles (optional)

White miniature marshmallows

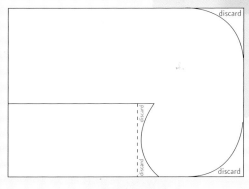

9 x 13-inch pan

SERVES: 10 to 12

star

PANS: 1 (8-inch) square pan

1 lemon or yellow cake mix

Light yellow frosting

Dark yellow or yellow-orange
 frosting

Yellow sprinkles

1. Make cake mix according to package directions. Pour batter into pan. Bake at 350 degrees F for 33 to 38 minutes. Cool cake in pan for 10 minutes, and then invert and cool completely on a wire rack.

2. Cut the cake according to the diagram and then, on a large serving platter or foil-wrapped board, position the two skinny top pieces to make the top point of the star. Flip over the fatter triangles and position to make the side points of the star. The side pieces will be pointing slightly upwards.

3. Frost the entire cake with light yellow frosting.

4. Using a star tip, outline the star with the dark yellow or yellow-orange frosting and then decorate the entire cake with yellow sprinkles.

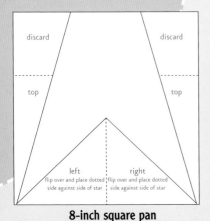

discard   discard

top   top

left   right
flip over and place dotted   flip over and place dotted
side against side of star   side against side of star

8-inch square pan

SERVES: 10 to 12

fuzzy mitten

PANS: 9 x 13-inch pan

1 cake mix, any flavor

White frosting

Light pink frosting

Shredded sweetened coconut

Multicolored decorator's balls

1. Make cake mix according to package directions. Pour batter into pan. Bake at 350 degrees F for 27 to 32 minutes and then carefully remove from oven. Cool cake in pan for 10 minutes, and then invert and cool completely on a wire rack.

2. Cut the cake according to the diagram and then place the mitten on a serving plate or foil-wrapped board. Discard or eat the leftover cake pieces.

3. Frost a strip across the bottom of the mitten white. Then frost the rest of the mitten light pink.

4. Completely cover the white frosting with the coconut, pressing lightly to secure.

5. Lightly sprinkle more coconut and decorator's balls over the pink frosting.

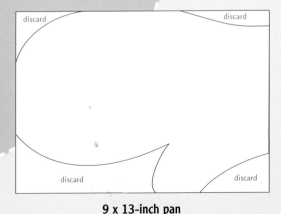

9 x 13-inch pan

SERVES: 10 to 12

wreath

1. Bake cake in a Bundt pan according to package directions. Carefully remove from the oven. Cool cake in pan for 10 minutes, and then invert and cool completely on a wire rack.

2. Place the cake on a serving plate or foil-wrapped board and frost entirely with light green frosting.

3. Using a decorator's bag with a star tip, make light green "pine needles" by slightly squeezing the bag to create each needle, starting in the center ring and working your way out. Squeeze the needles over the entire wreath, but don't worry about making them too close, as the spaces will be filled in.

4. Using another decorator's bag with the same size star tip and the dark green frosting, fill in any spaces so the entire cake is covered with pine needles.

5. Finish by making a bow with Fruit by the Foot at the top and gently pressing M&Ms into the frosting for holly berries.

PANS: Bundt pan

1 cake mix, any flavor

Light green frosting

Dark green frosting

Fruit by the Foot or red frosting

Red Peanut M&Ms

Bundt pan

SERVES: 10 to 12

red-nosed reindeer

PANS: 2 (9-inch) round pans

1 cake mix, any flavor

Light brown frosting

Dark brown frosting

White tube frosting

Dark brown M&Ms

Red tube frosting

1. Make cake in the prepared pans according to package directions. Carefully remove from the oven. Cool cake in pans for 10 minutes, and then invert and cool completely on a wire rack.

2. Cut the cakes according to the diagram. Place the cake on a large serving platter or foil-wrapped board to create the reindeer and his antlers.

3. Frost the reindeer's face and ears (part of the antler cake) with the light brown frosting.

4. Frost the antlers with the dark brown frosting.

5. Use the white tube frosting to create the reindeer's eyes and the dark brown frosting or M&Ms for his pupils. Finally, use the red frosting to make a big red nose.

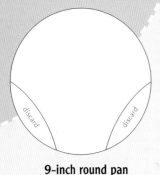

9-inch round pan

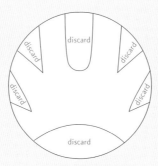

9-inch round pan

SERVES: 10 to 12

penguin

1. Make cake mix according to package directions. Fill two muffin cups two-thirds full and then pour remaining batter into the 9 x 13-inch pan. Bake at 350 degrees F for 17 to 20 minutes and then carefully remove cupcakes from oven. Bake other cake 12 to 15 minutes more. Cool cake in pan for 10 minutes, and then invert and cool completely on a wire rack.

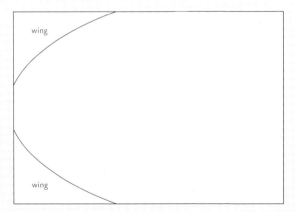

9 x 13-inch pan

2. Cut the cake according to the diagram. Place the cake on a large serving platter or foil-wrapped board to create the penguin and his wings.

PANS: Muffin pan
9 x 13-inch pan

1 cake mix, any flavor
Black frosting
White frosting
Yellow frosting

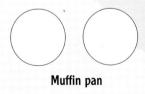

Muffin pan

SERVES: 10 to 12

3. Frost the wings and around the edge of the cake with the black frosting as shown in the picture. Fill in the center of the penguin with white frosting.

4. Completely frost the cupcakes with yellow frosting and then position as the penguin's feet.

5. Using a decorator's bag with a round tip and black frosting, outline the eyes and fill in the pupils. Use more yellow frosting to make the penguin's beak.

ornament

1. Make cake mix according to package directions. Pour batter into pan. Bake at 350 degrees F for 27 to 32 minutes and then carefully remove from oven. Cool cake in pan for 10 minutes, and then invert and cool completely on a wire rack.

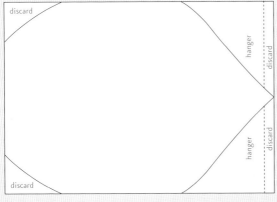

9 x 13-inch pan

2. Cut the cake according to the diagram. Place the cake on a large serving platter or foil-wrapped board to create the ornament, piecing the two larger cut pieces into a square at the top for the "hanger."

PANS: 9 x 13-inch pan

1 white cake mix, any flavor

White frosting

Bright green frosting

Bright pink sprinkles

Bright green sprinkles

1 piece green licorice

SERVES: 10 to 12

3. Frost the entire cake smoothly with white frosting.

4. Using a decorator's bag with a round tip and the bright green frosting, outline the pattern of the ornament.

5. Fill in the stripes and diamond shapes with the sprinkles as desired. Finish by sticking the green licorice into the top of the cake to make the hanger.

little gift

1. Make cake mixes according to package directions. Divide batter evenly between the prepared pans and bake for 33 to 38 minutes. Cool cakes in pans for 10 minutes and then cool completely on a wire rack.

2. Cover a piece of cardboard or a large cutting board with foil. Level each cake so that they can be stacked without wobbling.

3. Place one cake in the center of the board and frost the top with white frosting. Place the second cake on top and frost the entire cake white.

4. Position the Fruit by the Foot to look like ribbon and a bow around the gift.

2 (8-inch) square pans

5. Finish by making polka dots all over the cake with the M&Ms.

PANS: 2 (8-inch) square pans

2 white or chocolate
  cake mixes
White frosting
Red Fruit by the Foot
Red and green plain M&Ms

SERVES: 20 to 24

47

elf socks

PANS: 9 x 13-inch pan

1 cake mix, any flavor

Brown frosting

Pink frosting

2 Christmas Whoppers

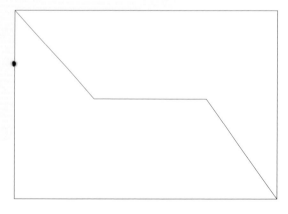

9 x 13-inch pan

1. Make cake mix according to package directions. Pour batter into pan. Bake at 350 degrees F for 27 to 32 minutes and then carefully remove from oven. Cool cake in pan for 10 minutes, and then invert and cool completely on a wire rack.

2. Cut the cake according to the diagram. On a serving plate or foil-wrapped board, position the two socks with the toes pointing out.

3. Very lightly frost each sock brown. Using two decorator's bags with the same size star tip, fill one bag with brown frosting and the other with pink frosting. Make stripes by doing rows of stars about 4 or 5 deep of each color. This will make the socks look like they were knitted.

4. Place a Christmas Whopper on the very tip of each toe.

SERVES: 10 to 12

the north pole

1. Make cake mix according to package directions. Spoon some batter into one muffin cup. Pour the rest of the batter into the square pan. Bake for 17 to 20 minutes and then carefully remove the cupcake from the oven. Bake the square cake another 15 to 18 minutes. Cool cake in pan for 10 minutes and then cool completely on a wire rack.

2. Cut the cake according to the diagram and then, on a large serving platter or foil-wrapped board, position the two long pieces end to end to create the pole.

3. Frost the entire pole smoothly with the white frosting. Use the red frosting to frost the cupcake at the top of the pole. Use the red frosting in a decorator's bag with a

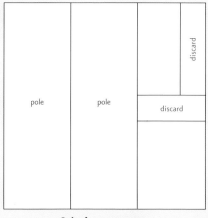

8-inch square pan

PANS: Muffin pan
1 (8-inch) square pan

1 cherry chip cake mix

White frosting

Red frosting

1 piece black licorice

Black tube frosting

Muffin pan

SERVES: 10 to 12

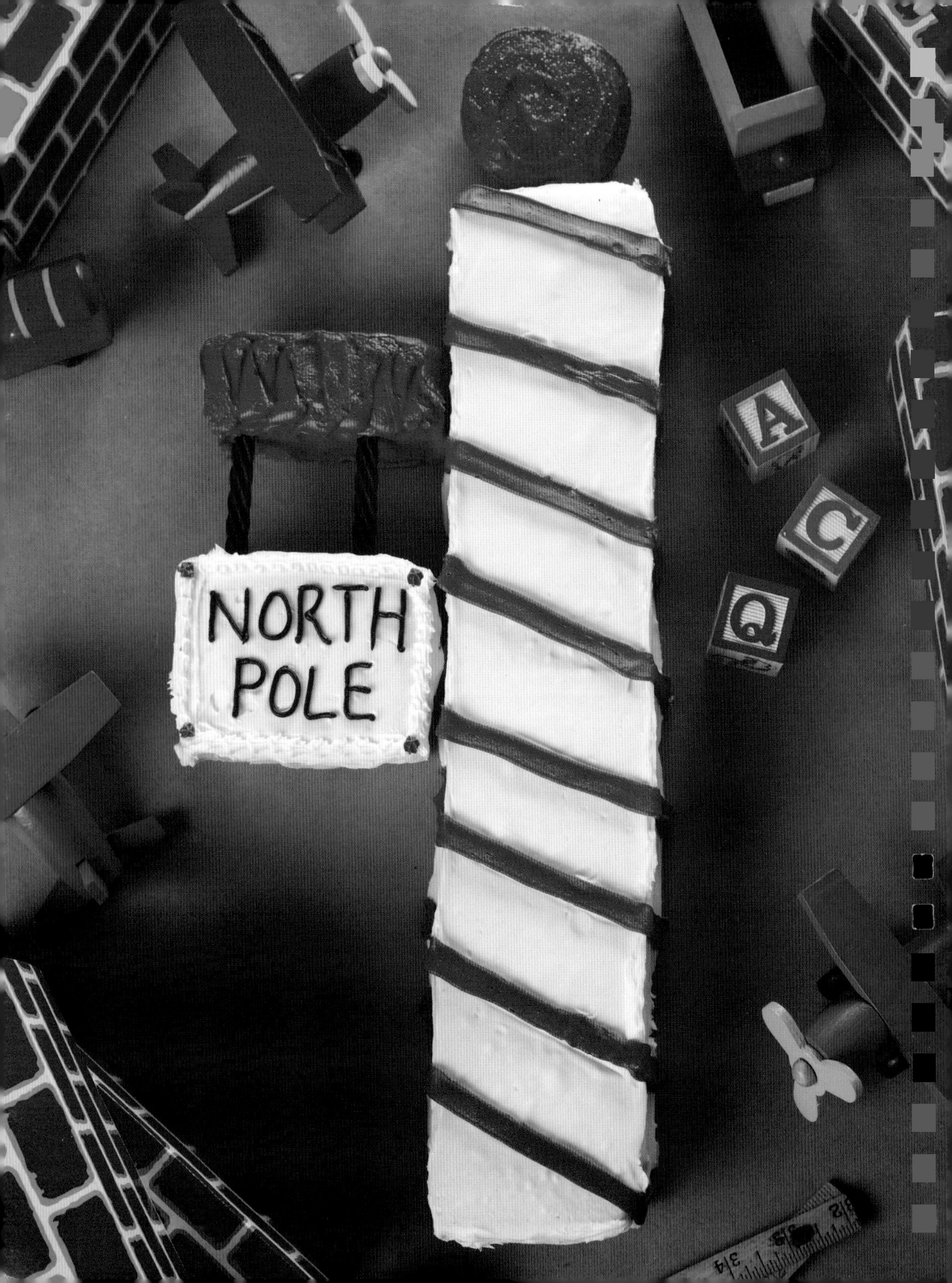
NORTH
POLE

round tip to draw the red lines that wrap around the pole. Let the lines dry a little and then flatten with your finger.

4. Frost the post attached to the pole with the red frosting and the sign with the white frosting.

5. Connect the sign to the post using pieces of the black licorice. Using the black tube frosting, draw the words "North Pole" on the sign.

old-fashioned christmas lightbulb

PANS: 9 x 13-inch pan

1 cake mix, any flavor

Red frosting

Black frosting

Black licorice

1. Make cake mix according to package directions. Pour batter into pan. Bake at 350 degrees F for 27 to 32 minutes and then carefully remove from oven. Cool cake in pan for 10 minutes and then invert and cool completely on a wire rack.

2. Cut the cake according to the diagram. On a serving plate, position the two oblong triangle pieces together to make a square (you may have to cut them a little so they fit together to make a rectangle). Position at the bottom of the lightbulb.

3. Frost the lightbulb smoothly with the red frosting and the square at the bottom with the black frosting.

4. Cut licorice to same length as rectangle on bottom of the light bulb and place on top to make the threads.

Variation: Make the lightbulb your favorite color and add some sparkly sprinkles!

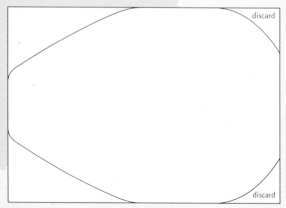

discard

discard

9 x 13-inch pan

SERVES: 10 to 12

holly berry

1. Make cake mix according to package directions. Fill three muffin cups three-fourths full of cake batter and then pour remaining batter into cake pan. Bake at 350 degrees F for 17 to 20 minutes and then carefully remove the cupcakes from the oven. Bake the square cake 10 to 15 minutes more and remove from oven. Cool cake in pan for 10 minutes and then invert and cool completely on a wire rack.

2. Cut the square cake according to the diagram. Place the cupcakes on your cake plate or foil-wrapped board to look like the holly berries and the cut cake to look like the leaves.

3. Frost the cupcakes red and the leaves light green. Outline the leaves with the dark green or gel frosting.

PANS: Muffin pan
1 (8-inch) square pan

1 cake mix, any flavor

Red frosting

Light green frosting

Dark green frosting or 1 tube green gel frosting

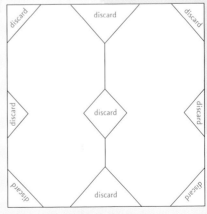

1 (8-inch) square pan

SERVES: 10 to 12

gingerbread house

PANS: 2 (8-inch) square pans

1 cake mix, any flavor

White frosting

Brown or light brown frosting

4 graham crackers

Christmas candies

1. Make cake mix according to package directions. Pour two-thirds of the batter into one pan and the remaining third into the other pan. This will make one cake twice as thick as the other. Bake at 350 degrees F for 18 to 20 minutes and then carefully remove the thinner cake from the oven. Bake the larger cake 10 to 12 minutes more and then remove from oven. Cool cake in pans for 10 minutes and then invert and cool completely on a wire rack.

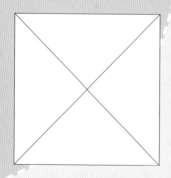

8-inch square pan

8-inch square pan

2. Cut the thinner cake into triangles according to the diagram, making sure it is level and lays flat. Cut the thicker cake according to the diagram and level, then stack the two long rectangles on a cake plate, frosting between the layers. Frost together the thin triangles with white frosting and reinforce with toothpicks if necessary so they stay together. Place on top of rectangle layers to make the roof.

SERVES: 10 to 12

3. Frost the rooftop with white frosting and the rest of the cake with brown frosting. Place the graham crackers on top of the roof and then frost a thick layer of white frosting over the crackers, making sure to cover all the edges.

4. Using a decorator's bag with a wide round tip, draw a white line of frosting at the very peak of the roof to "connect" the graham crackers. You may also want to go around the edges of the graham crackers as well so you can stick candy all around the roof's edges.

5. Draw lines of frosting around all edges of the house and then decorate the cake as you would a gingerbread house, using Christmas candies.

polar bear

1. Make cake mix according to package directions. Fill three cups of the cupcake pan about two-thirds full. Grease the mixing bowl well and pour remaining batter into the bowl. Bake cupcakes and cake at 350 degrees F for 18 to 22 minutes. Remove cupcakes without disturbing the cake. Bake cake another 25 to 30 minutes. Test with a wooden skewer inserted in the center. If it comes out clean, the cake is done. Cool cake in bowl for 10 minutes and then invert and cool completely on a wire rack.

1 (2.5-quart) glass mixing bowl   3 muffins

PANS: Muffin pan
1 (2.5-quart) glass mixing bowl

1 cake mix, any flavor

White frosting

1 tube blue or red frosting

1 tube black or black gel frosting

Red rope licorice or 1 tube red or red gel frosting

2 Oreo cookies

2 blue M&Ms

Red Fruit by the Foot

SERVES: 10 to 12

2. On a serving plate or foil-wrapped board, position the round cake flat-side-down and two cupcakes at the top to create the bear's face and ears.

3. Frost all sides of two cupcakes as well as the rest of the cake with white frosting. Slice off the top of the remaining cupcake and place it slightly below the middle center of the bear's head to create the nose. Frost and blend the sides of the cupcake into the bear's face with white frosting.

4. Using the blue or red tube frosting, fill in a circle in the middle of each ear. Using the black or black gel frosting, draw a nose on the cupcake top. Use red rope licorice or red frosting to make the mouth.

5. Separate two Oreos and place just above the cupcake nose, with the cream filling face up, to make the eyes. Use the black frosting or blue M&Ms to make the pupils and then form a bow tie out of the Fruit by the Foot.

santa

1 cake mix, any flavor

White frosting

Light pink or peach frosting

Red frosting

Black frosting

Shredded coconut or mini
  marshmallows

Red tube frosting

1. Make cake mix according to package directions. Pour batter into pan. Bake at 350 degrees F for 27 to 32 minutes and then carefully remove from oven. Cool cake in pan for 10 minutes and then invert and cool completely on a wire rack.

2. Cut the cake according to the diagram. Place one of the triangle pieces at the top of a large serving platter or foil-wrapped board to create Santa's hat. Place the rectangle piece underneath for Santa's face, and the other triangle piece below that to make his beard.

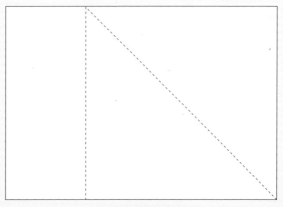

9 x 13-inch pan

SERVES: 10 to 12

3. Frost Santa's entire beard white, along with a strip of white at the bottom of his hat. Frost his face pink or peach and his hat red.

4. Using a decorator's bag with a small round tip filled with black frosting, draw Santa's eyes and nose.

5. Finish decorating by pressing coconut or mini marshmallows all over the white frosting and use the red tube frosting to draw Santa's mouth.

about the author

Melissa Barlow received her bachelor's degree in journalism from Weber State University. She is a freelance writer and editor. She also has formal training in cake decorating. Melissa is the author of *Easy Cut-Up Cakes for Kids* and co-author of the books *101 Things To Do With a Salad* and *101 Things To Do With Gelatin*. She lives with her husband, Todd, in Bountiful, Utah.

Taste of Home

simple &

delicious

COOKBOOK

Taste of Home
B O O K S

REIMAN MEDIA GROUP, INC. • GREENDALE, WISCONSIN

A TASTE OF HOME/READER'S DIGEST BOOK

Editors: Jean Steiner, Jennifer Olski
Art Director: Edwin Robles, Jr.
Layout Designer: Catherine Fletcher
Proofreader: Linne Bruskewitz
Editorial Assistant: Barb Czysz
Food Director: Diane Werner RD
Recipe Testing and Editing: Taste of Home Test Kitchen
Food Photography: Reiman Photo Studio
Cover Photo Photographer: Jim Wieland
Cover Food Stylist: Sarah Thompson
Cover Set Stylist: Dolores Schaefer

Senior Editor, Retail Books: Jennifer Olski
Vice President/Executive Editor, Books: Heidi Reuter Lloyd
Creative Director: Ardyth Cope
Senior Vice President/Editor in Chief: Catherine Cassidy
President and Chief Executive Officer: Mary G. Berner
President, Food & Entertaining: Suzanne M. Grimes

International Standard Book Number (10): 0-89821-684-2
International Standard Book Number (13): 978-0-89821-684-4
Library of Congress Control Number: 2007938812

For other Taste of Home books and products,
visit www.tasteofhome.com.
For more Reader's Digest products and information, visit
www.rd.com (in the United States)
www.rd.ca (in Canada)

PRINTED IN CHINA
1 3 5 7 9 10 8 6 4 2

table of contents

pg. 198

pg. 128

pg. 166

introduction

Weekday cooking is truly simple and delicious with this book's planned-out menus and handy grocery lists. Plus, food shopping will be a breeze!

Fuss-free meals week after week...

Preparing delicious weekday meals your family will love can be so simple. All you really need is a plan, and that's exactly what this **Simple & Delicious Cookbook** provides!

Every home cook knows that entrees are the key to meal planning. Our Test Kitchen home economists have done that time-consuming planning for you by putting together 12 weeks of easy, family-pleasing main dishes—that's 60 recipes! And to save you even more time, they've also created weekly shopping lists of the ingredients you'll need to make the dishes! (Look for the Weekday Meals starting on page 7.)

To round out these menus, this handy cookbook also features Breakfast, Soups & Sandwiches, Salads & Sides, and Desserts chapters full of appealing partners—mix and match them any way you wish to suit your family's tastes.

With **Simple & Delicious**, you'll have everything you need for fuss-free meals week after week!

Mix and Match

With 182 appealing partners in
the second half of this book, it's
easy to round out your menus.
First, pick an appetizing main
dish or sandwich. Then, flip to
soups, salads or sides for the
perfect match. Finally, browse
the desserts for a delectable
ending. With so many tantalizing
options to choose from, you'll
never run out of great new
meal ideas.

+

or

+

or

Chock-full of helpful tips

Many recipes in this cookbook feature a timely tip,
such as tricks that reduce preparation time, facts for
buying and storing foods, or substitution secrets. So
be sure to watch for this helpful tip icon.

Recipes keep time in mind

Most of this cookbook's recipes go from start to finish in less
than 30 minutes—some in just 20 or 10! Handy time icons
like those pictured at right identify these quick-to-fix recipes
throughout the book. You'll also find preparation and cooking
times for every recipe prominently displayed.

Food Staples List

Try to keep these items on hand to speed up the preparation of the weekday meals (and most other recipes) in this cookbook:

- All-purpose flour
- Bay leaf
- Beef broth or beef bouillon
- Biscuit/baking mix
- Brown sugar
- Butter
- Cajun seasoning
- Canola oil
- Cayenne pepper
- Chicken broth or chicken bouillon
- Cider vinegar
- Cornstarch
- Creamy peanut butter
- Crushed red pepper flakes
- Dijon mustard
- Dill weed
- Dried basil
- Dried oregano
- Dried parsley flakes
- Dried rosemary

- Dried thyme
- Eggs
- Garlic cloves or minced garlic
- Garlic powder
- Grated Parmesan cheese
- Ground allspice
- Ground cinnamon
- Ground ginger
- Ground mustard
- Ground nutmeg
- Honey
- Hot pepper sauce
- Italian seasoning
- Ketchup
- Lemon juice
- Lemon-pepper seasoning
- Mayonnaise
- Milk
- Olive oil
- Onion

- Paprika
- Pasta (a variety of dried kinds)
- Pepper
- Plain dry bread crumbs
- Prepared mustard
- Red wine vinegar
- Rice
- Rubbed sage
- Salt
- Seasoned bread crumbs
- Soy sauce
- Stone-ground mustard
- Sugar
- Vegetable oil
- White pepper
- White wine
- White wine vinegar
- Worcestershire sauce
- Yellow cornmeal

Food Storage Pointers

Check the sell-by or use-by dates on pantry items. Throw out any items that are past those dates. Store opened items tightly closed and place in a cool, dry place.

The use-by date on refrigerated items is only for the unopened item. Be sure to keep your fridge's temperature between 34° and 40°. Store leftovers in covered refrigerator containers or wrap them in plastic wrap or foil; resealable plastic bags also are great for storage.

week one

Monday's Dish
Salsa Fish, pg. 8

tues. *wed.* *thurs.* *fri.*

shopping list

- ○ 4 boneless skinless chicken breast halves (4 ounces *each*)
- ○ 2 pounds ground beef
- ○ 6 boneless pork loin chops (8 ounces *each*)
- ○ 4 boneless rib eye steaks (6 ounces *each*)
- ○ 2 pounds walleye, bass *or* perch fillets
- ○ 1/2 cup white wine
- ○ 1 envelope taco seasoning
- ○ 1 can (14-1/2 ounces) diced tomatoes with onions
- ○ 1 can (11-1/2 ounces) condensed bean with bacon soup
- ○ 1 can (21 ounces) apple pie filling
- ○ 12 gingersnaps
- ○ 2 cups unsweetened apple juice
- ○ 1 tablespoon baking cocoa
- ○ 1 tablespoon instant coffee granules
- ○ 1-1/2 cups salsa
- ○ 1/2 cup shredded cheddar cheese
- ○ 2 cups (8 ounces) shredded part-skim mozzarella cheese

STAPLES FOR THE WEEK

- ❏ Garlic cloves *or* prepared minced garlic
- ❏ Salt
- ❏ Pepper
- ❏ Dried basil
- ❏ Dried oregano
- ❏ Paprika
- ❏ Ground allspice
- ❏ Vegetable oil
- ❏ Butter
- ❏ Chicken broth *or* chicken bouillon
- ❏ Flour
- ❏ Cornstarch
- ❏ Seasoned bread crumbs
- ❏ Plain dry bread crumbs
- ❏ Brown sugar

Easy-does-it dining means less stress!

It's hard to say who will be more impressed by this weeknight dinner plan: your family when they sit down to scrumptious meals like these every night...or you when you wrap up meal prep in record time! For perfect endings to these delectable dinners, check out the delicious dessert options starting on page 193. Don't forget to shop ahead for those treats, too!

My family loves outdoor activities, especially fishing. I give their catch of the day unexpected zip with salsa. It dresses up these golden, crumb-coated fillets and keeps them both moist and tender.
—Diane Grajewski
North Branch, Michigan

㉑ Salsa Fish

prep/total time: 20 min.

    2 pounds walleye, bass *or* perch fillets
    1 cup seasoned bread crumbs
    1 tablespoon vegetable oil
1-1/2 cups salsa
    2 cups (8 ounces) shredded part-skim mozzarella cheese

Coat fillets with bread crumbs. In a large skillet, brown fillets on both sides in oil. Transfer to a greased 13-in. x 9-in. x 2-in. baking dish. Top with the salsa and cheese. Bake, uncovered, at 400° for 7-10 minutes or until fish flakes easily with a fork and the cheese is melted. **Yield:** 6 servings.

Make It Italian (tip)

To give this fish an Italian twist, substitute spaghetti sauce for the salsa. Then serve the flaky fish over buttered pasta.

This one-skillet chicken and gravy dish that's ready to serve in less than 30 minutes is sure to become a family favorite.
—Taste of Home Test Kitchen

(tip) **Peeling And Chopping Garlic:** Place garlic cloves on a cutting board. With the flat side of a chef's knife, press down until you hear the peel crack; remove and discard peel. Coarsely chop the garlic.

Cider-Glazed Carrots, pg. 150

Garlic Chicken 'n' Gravy (30)

prep/total time: 25 min.

4 boneless skinless chicken breast halves (4 ounces *each*)
1/4 teaspoon salt
1/4 teaspoon pepper
5 garlic cloves, peeled and chopped
2 tablespoons butter
1/2 cup plus 2 tablespoons chicken broth, *divided*
1/2 cup white wine *or* additional broth
1/2 teaspoon dried basil
1/4 teaspoon dried oregano
1 tablespoon all-purpose flour

Sprinkle chicken with salt and pepper. In a large skillet, cook chicken and garlic in butter over medium-high heat for 5 minutes or until browned. Add 1/2 cup broth, wine or additional broth, basil and oregano. Bring to a boil. Reduce heat; cover and simmer for 7-9 minutes or until chicken is no longer pink.

Remove chicken with a slotted spoon and keep warm. In a small bowl, combine flour and remaining broth until smooth; stir into pan juices. Bring to a boil; cook and stir for 1-2 minutes or until thickened. Serve over chicken. **Yield:** 4 servings.

A gingersnap-apple filling makes these stuffed pork chops a special weeknight meal. You'll never prepare plain pork chops again!
—Taste of Home Test Kitchen

Sesame Green Beans, pg. 175

Ginger-Apple Pork Chops

prep: 15 min. **bake:** 25 min.

6 boneless pork loin chops (1 inch thick and 8 ounces *each*)
1 teaspoon salt
1/2 teaspoon pepper
1 tablespoon vegetable oil
1 can (21 ounces) apple pie filling
12 gingersnaps, crumbled
2 tablespoons cornstarch
2 cups unsweetened apple juice

Cut a pocket in each pork chop. Sprinkle with salt and pepper. In a large skillet, brown chops in oil on both sides. Cool for 5 minutes.

Combine the pie filling and gingersnaps; stuff some of the mixture into the pocket of each pork chop. Set the remaining mixture aside.

Secure pork with toothpicks. Place in a greased 15-in. x 10-in. x 1-in. baking pan. Cover and bake at 350° for 25-30 minutes or until a meat thermometer reads 160°. Discard toothpicks.

In a small saucepan, combine cornstarch and apple juice until smooth. Stir in the reserved pie filling mixture. Bring to a boil; cook and stir for 1 minute or until thickened. Serve over pork chops. **Yield:** 6 servings.

Simmering browned beef patties in bean with bacon soup and diced tomatoes makes a moist and tasty burger!
—Taste of Home Test Kitchen

- - - - - - - - - - - -

tip **Quick Corn on The Cob:** These burgers need only a simple side dish to make a mouth-watering meal. Here's a quick way to make corn on the cob. Place 6 small ears of fresh corn in a Dutch oven of boiling water. Cook for 3 to 5 minutes or until tender; drain.

Southwestern Skillet Burgers ⏱30

prep/total time: 30 min.

2 pounds ground beef
1/2 cup dry bread crumbs
1 envelope taco seasoning
1 can (14-1/2 ounces) diced tomatoes with onions, undrained
1 can (11-1/2 ounces) condensed bean with bacon soup, undiluted
1/2 cup shredded cheddar cheese

In a bowl, combine the beef, bread crumbs and taco seasoning. Shape into six 3/4-in.-thick patties. In a large skillet over medium heat, cook patties for 3 minutes on each side or until browned. Remove patties; drain.

Add tomatoes and soup to the skillet; return patties to the pan. Bring to a boil. Reduce heat; cover and simmer for 10 minutes or until the meat is no longer pink. Sprinkle with cheese; cover and heat until cheese is melted. **Yield:** 6 servings.

This rub recipe is wonderful on boneless rib eye steaks, but you could also use it on any other kind of thin-cut steaks.
—*Taste of Home Test Kitchen*

- - - - - - - - - - - - -

Shopping **(tip)**
For
Steak:
Choose steaks with a bright, cherry red color that are firm to the touch, not soft.

Grilled Rib Eyes

prep: 10 min. + marinating **grill:** 10 min.

2 tablespoons brown sugar
1 tablespoon baking cocoa
1 tablespoon instant coffee granules, finely crushed
1 teaspoon paprika
1/2 teaspoon salt
1/2 teaspoon ground allspice
1/2 teaspoon pepper
4 boneless rib eye steaks (6 ounces *each*)

In a small bowl, combine the first seven ingredients. Rub over both sides of steaks. Refrigerate for 1 hour.

Grill steaks, uncovered, over medium-hot heat for 5-8 minutes on each side or until meat reaches desired doneness (for medium-rare, a meat thermometer should read 145°; medium, 160°; well-done, 170°). **Yield:** 4 servings.

Wednesday's Dish
Taco Puffs, pg. 16

mon. tues. thurs. fri.

shopping list

- ○ 2 packages (20 ounces *each*) boneless turkey tenderloins
- ○ 4 orange roughy fillets (6 ounces *each*)
- ○ 4 boneless skinless chicken breast halves (4 ounces *each*)
- ○ 1 pound ground beef
- ○ 4 bone-in pork loin chops (1/2 inch thick and 6 ounces *each*)
- ○ 3/4 cup finely chopped pecans
- ○ 1 tablespoon chopped shallot
- ○ 1/2 cup white wine
- ○ 1 cup orange juice
- ○ 1 medium green pepper
- ○ 4 sandwich buns
- ○ 1 can (15 ounces) apricot halves
- ○ 1/4 cup apricot preserves
- ○ 4 green onions, chopped
- ○ 1 envelope taco seasoning
- ○ 2 tubes large refrigerated flaky biscuits
- ○ 8 ounces cheddar cheese slices *or* 2 cups (8 ounces) shredded cheddar cheese
- ○ 1 bottle (12 ounces) chili sauce

STAPLES FOR THE WEEK

- ❒ Onion
- ❒ Salt
- ❒ Pepper
- ❒ Eggs
- ❒ Butter
- ❒ Cornstarch
- ❒ White wine vineger
- ❒ Dijon mustard
- ❒ Prepared mustard
- ❒ Ketchup
- ❒ Chicken broth *or* chicken bouillon
- ❒ Worchestershire sauce
- ❒ Hot pepper sauce
- ❒ Rice

Shopping shortcuts save kitchen time...

When you head to the market this week, scout out the frozen food section for time-saving meal helpers. Pick up packages of frozen chopped onions and green peppers for easy measuring. Grab an extra bag of mixed greens for a simple side salad. And swing by the bakery for a big loaf of French bread to serve alongside a meal or use instead of sandwich buns.

I often accompany this dish with mashed potatoes and serve the chili sauce as gravy. This meal is easy to make after a long day.
—Nicole Svacina
St. Nazianz,
Wisconsin

30 Chili Chops

prep/total time: 30 min.

4 **bone-in pork loin chops (1/2 inch thick and 6 ounces** *each***)**
4 **slices onion (1/4 inch thick)**
4 **slices green pepper (1/4 inch thick)**
1 **bottle (12 ounces) chili sauce**

Place the pork chops in a greased 9-in. square baking dish. Top with the onion, green pepper and chili sauce. Cover and bake at 350° for 20-30 minutes or until meat juices run clear. **Yield:** 4 servings.

Picking Out Pork Chops

Pork chop meat should be reddish pink. Avoid cutlets that have a brown or greenish tinge. Keep raw pork chops in their original wrapping and store in the refrigerator for 2 to 3 days or freeze for up to 6 months.

Canned apricots add color and nutrition to this delicious fruit sauce served over quick-cooking chicken breasts.
—Taste of Home Test Kitchen

(tip) **No-Fuss Slicing:** Once the apricots are drained, slice the halves right in the can by running a knife back and forth inside the can until all the halves are sliced.

Apricot Chicken ㉚

prep/total time: 25 min.

4 boneless skinless chicken breast
   halves (4 ounces *each*)
1/4 teaspoon salt
1/4 teaspoon pepper
2 tablespoons butter
1 can (15 ounces) apricot halves
3 teaspoons cornstarch
1/4 cup apricot preserves
2 tablespoons white wine vinegar
4 green onions, chopped
Hot cooked rice, optional

Sprinkle chicken with salt and pepper. In a large skillet, cook chicken in butter over medium heat for 5 minutes, turning occasionally. Cover and cook 5 minutes longer or until juices run clear. Remove and keep warm.

Drain apricots, reserving juice. Cut apricots into 1/2-in. slices; set aside. In a small bowl, combine cornstarch and reserved juice until smooth. Stir in preserves and vinegar until combined; pour into skillet. Bring to a boil over medium heat; cook and stir for 1-2 minutes or until thickened. Add apricots and chicken; heat through. Sprinkle with onions. Serve with rice if desired. **Yield:** 4 servings.

I got this recipe years ago and still make the cheesy sandwiches often.
—*Jan Schmid Hibbing, Minnesota*

Freeze It: **tip** If your family favors Mexican food, keep taco meat in the freezer. Cook 3 pounds ground beef and 1-1/2 cups chopped onion over medium heat until meat is no longer pink; drain. Add 3 envelopes taco seasoning and prepare according to directions. Cool and freeze in 1-pound portions.

30 Taco Puffs

prep/total time: 30 min.

1 **pound ground beef**
1/2 **cup chopped onion**
1 **envelope taco seasoning**
2 **tubes (16.3 ounces *each*) large refrigerated flaky biscuits**
8 **ounces cheddar cheese slices *or* 2 cups (8 ounces) shredded cheddar cheese**

In a large skillet, cook beef and onion over medium heat until meat is no longer pink; drain. Add the taco seasoning and prepare according to package directions. Cool slightly.

Flatten half of the biscuits into 4-in. circles; place in greased 15-in. x 10-in. x 1-in. baking pans. Spoon 1/4 cup meat mixture onto each; top with two cheese slices or 1/4 cup shredded cheese. Flatten remaining biscuits; place on top and pinch edges to seal tightly. Bake at 400° for 15 minutes or until golden brown. **Yield:** 8 servings.

The spicy sauce for these speedy turkey sandwiches is so quick to stir together because it uses convenience foods such as mustard, ketchup and hot pepper sauce.
—Mrs. Johnye Masteres
Rayville, Louisiana

(tip) **Cooking Turkey:** Simmer the turkey tenderloins you picked up at the grocery store this week in chicken broth until a meat thermometer reads 170°. Cool and cube 3 cups for this recipe.

Saucy Turkey ㉚
prep/total time: 30 min.

1/2 cup chopped green pepper
1/3 cup chopped onion
2 tablespoons butter
1-1/2 cups ketchup
1/2 cup chicken broth
1-1/2 teaspoons Worcestershire sauce
1 teaspoon prepared mustard
1/4 to 1/2 teaspoon hot pepper sauce
1/4 teaspoon pepper
3 cups cubed cooked turkey
4 sandwich buns, split

In a large saucepan, saute the green pepper and onion in butter until tender. Stir in the ketchup, broth, Worcestershire sauce, mustard, hot pepper sauce and pepper. Add turkey. Simmer, uncovered, for 20 minutes or until heated through. Serve on buns. **Yield:** 4 servings.

A few minutes is all you need to prepare this nut-coated fish, but your family will think you fussed! Any white fish fillets, like ocean perch, cod, haddock, pollock or red snapper, can be substituted for orange roughy.
—Taste of Home Test Kitchen

30 Pecan-Coated Roughy

prep/total time: 30 min.

1 egg, lightly beaten
3/4 cup finely chopped pecans
4 orange roughy fillets (6 ounces each)
1 tablespoon chopped shallot
2 teaspoons butter
1/2 cup white wine
2 teaspoons cornstarch
1 cup orange juice
2 teaspoons Dijon mustard

Place the egg and pecans in separate shallow bowls. Dip fillets into egg, then coat with pecans. Place in a greased 15-in. x 10-in. x 1-in. baking pan. Bake, uncovered, at 400° for 20-25 minutes or until fish flakes easily with a fork.

Meanwhile, in a small saucepan, saute shallot in butter until tender. Add wine. Bring to a boil; cook for 1-2 minutes or until liquid is reduced by half. In a small bowl, combine the cornstarch, orange juice and mustard until smooth; stir into wine mixture. Bring to a boil; cook and stir for 2 minutes or until thickened. Serve with orange roughy. **Yield:** 4 servings.

Friday's Dish
Chicken Satay Wraps, pg. 24

mon tues wed thurs

shopping list

- ○ 1 package (17 ounces) refrigerated beef tips with gravy
- ○ 1 deli rotisserie chicken
- ○ 4 bone-in pork loin chops (1/2 inch thick and 6 ounces *each*)
- ○ 1 pound sea scallops
- ○ 1 package (14 ounces) frozen sugar snap peas
- ○ 2 medium tomatoes
- ○ 1 cup cherry tomatoes
- ○ 1 cup sliced fresh mushrooms
- ○ 1/2 cup prepared pesto
- ○ 2 green onions
- ○ 1 cup coleslaw mix
- ○ 4 flour tortillas (8 inches)
- ○ 1 pound white cheddar cheese
- ○ 1 carton (8 ounces) spreadable chive and onion cream cheese

STAPLES FOR THE WEEK

- ❑ Onion
- ❑ Vegetable oil
- ❑ Olive oil
- ❑ Salt
- ❑ Pepper
- ❑ White pepper
- ❑ Ground mustard
- ❑ Flour
- ❑ Butter
- ❑ Milk
- ❑ Eggs
- ❑ Seasoned bread crumbs
- ❑ Creamy peanut butter
- ❑ Chicken broth *or* chicken bouillon
- ❑ Soy sauce
- ❑ Pasta (penne, linguine and angel hair)

Use your noodle for meal magic!

Linguine, penne, angel hair, macaroni, spaghetti, rigatoni...there are oodles of noodles you can use for these main dishes. To cook any pasta more evenly, prevent it from sticking together and avoid boil-overs, always use a large kettle. Stir noodles within the first minute after adding to boiling water. Cook just until firm, yet tender. Then immediately drain, shake to remove excess water and toss with sauce or butter while still hot!

Chive and onion cream cheese makes a delicious sauce for these baked pork loin chops.
—Taste of Home Test Kitchen

Freezing Chicken Broth: **(tip)**
After opening a can of ready-to-use chicken broth for this recipe, freeze the rest in 1/2-cup portions and save for future use.

⏱ **30** Breaded Pork Chops

prep/total time: 30 min.

1 egg
3/4 cup seasoned bread crumbs
4 bone-in pork loin chops (1/2 inch thick and 6 ounces *each*)
1 carton (8 ounces) spreadable chive and onion cream cheese
3 tablespoons chicken broth
2 tablespoons milk

In a shallow bowl, beat the egg. Place the bread crumbs in another shallow bowl. Dip pork chops into egg, then coat with crumbs. Place in a greased 15-in. x 10-in. x 1-in. baking pan. Bake, uncovered, at 350° for 25-30 minutes or until a meat thermometer reads 160°.

In a small saucepan, combine the cream cheese, broth and milk. Cook and stir over medium heat for 5 minutes or until smooth and blended. Serve with pork chops. **Yield:** 4 servings.

This recipe deliciously tops off pasta with sea scallops, which can range from 1/2 to 1 inch thick. To cook thicker scallops more quickly, cut them in half horizontally.
—Taste of Home Test Kitchen

Scallop Pesto Pasta ⏱30

prep/total time: 25 min.

8 ounces uncooked angel hair pasta
1/2 cup all-purpose flour
1/2 teaspoon salt
1/4 teaspoon pepper
1 pound sea scallops
3 tablespoons butter
1/2 cup prepared pesto

Cook pasta according to package directions. Meanwhile, in a large resealable plastic bag, combine the flour, salt and pepper; add scallops and shake to coat. In a large skillet, cook scallops in butter for 2-1/2 to 3 minutes on each side or until opaque. Drain pasta; toss with pesto. Top with scallops. **Yield:** 4 servings.

Cooking with Scallops (tip)

Frozen scallops should be kept frozen until just before cooking. Thaw them in the refrigerator or by putting them in a colander and running cold water over them. Fresh scallops should be refrigerated and used within 2 days of purchase.

Put away that packaged mix! Here, white cheddar cheese and tomatoes add a whole new dimension to macaroni and cheese.
—*Taste of Home Test Kitchen*

- - - - - - - - - - - - -

Seeding Tomatoes: (*tip*) To remove tomato seeds, cut a tomato in half horizontally and remove the stem. Holding half over a bowl or sink, scrape out the seeds with a small spoon, or squeeze to force out the seeds.

⏱ **30** Tomato Mac 'n' Cheese

prep/total time: 30 min.

1 package (12 ounces) uncooked penne pasta
3 tablespoons butter
3 tablespoons all-purpose flour
3 cups milk
1 pound white cheddar cheese, shredded
1/2 teaspoon salt
1/2 teaspoon ground mustard
1/4 teaspoon white pepper
1 cup chopped seeded tomatoes

Cook the pasta according to package directions. Meanwhile, in a Dutch oven, melt butter over medium heat. Stir in flour until smooth; gradually add the milk. Bring to a boil; cook and stir for 2 minutes or until thickened.

Reduce heat to medium. Stir in the cheese, salt, mustard and pepper. Cook and stir until cheese is melted. Drain pasta; stir into cheese sauce. Cook and stir for 3 minutes or until heated through. Stir in tomatoes just until combined. **Yield:** 8 servings.

Add any other of your favorite vegetables to this tasty recipe for a quick and delicious meal, or serve it over instant white or brown rice instead of pasta.
—Taste of Home Test Kitchen

Vegetable Beef Ragout

prep/total time: 20 min.

1 cup sliced fresh mushrooms
1/2 cup chopped onion
1 tablespoon vegetable oil
1 package (17 ounces) refrigerated beef tips with gravy
1 package (14 ounces) frozen sugar snap peas, thawed
1 cup cherry tomatoes, halved
Hot cooked pasta, optional

In a large skillet, saute mushrooms and onion in oil until tender. Add the beef tips with gravy, peas and tomatoes; heat through. Serve over pasta if desired. **Yield:** 4 servings.

Where to Buy Beef Tips (tip)

Refrigerated beef tips with gravy can be found in the meat section of your grocery store. Reheat according to package directions and serve over refrigerated mashed potatoes. Better yet, jazz up the beef tips by following this easy recipe!

Rotisserie chicken or refrigerated grilled chicken strips can be used to speed up the preparation of this recipe. Whole wheat, spinach or sun-dried tomato tortillas are a nice change of pace from traditional flour tortillas.
—Taste of Home Test Kitchen

Chicken Satay Wraps

prep/total time: 15 min.

- 2 tablespoons olive oil
- 2 tablespoons creamy peanut butter
- 2 green onions, chopped
- 1 teaspoon soy sauce
- 1/4 teaspoon pepper
- 2 cups sliced cooked chicken
- 1 cup coleslaw mix
- 4 flour tortillas (8 inches), warmed

In a large bowl, whisk the oil, peanut butter, onions, soy sauce and pepper until combined. Add the chicken and toss to coat. Sprinkle 1/4 cup coleslaw mix over each tortilla; top with the chicken mixture. Roll up tightly. **Yield:** 4 servings.

What Is Satay? (tip)

Satay (sah-TAY) is an Indonesian favorite usually prepared as an appetizer consisting of cubes of marinated meat, fish or poultry threaded on skewers and grilled or broiled. Satay is typically served with a spicy peanut sauce.

week four

shopping list

- ○ 1 package (20 ounces) turkey breast tenderloins
- ○ 4 catfish fillets (6 ounces *each*)
- ○ 1-1/2 pounds boneless skinless chicken breast halves
- ○ 5 Italian sausage links
- ○ 1 pound ground beef
- ○ 1 package (10 ounces) fresh spinach
- ○ 1 fresh lemon
- ○ 1/2 cup sliced celery
- ○ 1/2 cup sliced carrots
- ○ 3 medium yellow summer squash
- ○ 1 medium green pepper
- ○ 1 package (20 ounces) refrigerated cheese tortellini
- ○ 1/2 cup white wine
- ○ 1 jar (15-1/2 ounces) roasted sweet red peppers
- ○ 1 can (15 ounces) pizza sauce
- ○ 1 can (14-1/2 ounces) diced tomatoes
- ○ 1 can (8 ounces) tomato sauce
- ○ 1 cup (4 ounces) shredded part-skim mozzarella cheese
- ○ 1 cup (4 ounces) shredded Parmesan cheese
- ○ 3 cups (12 ounces) shredded Swiss cheese

STAPLES FOR THE WEEK

- ❏ Garlic cloves *or* prepared minced garlic
- ❏ Salt
- ❏ Pepper
- ❏ Olive oil
- ❏ Vegetable oil
- ❏ Flour
- ❏ Chicken broth (three 14-1/2 ounce cans) *or* chicken bouillon
- ❏ Beef broth (one 14-1/2 ounce can) *or* beef bouillon
- ❏ Milk
- ❏ Eggs
- ❏ Yellow cornmeal
- ❏ Biscuit/baking mix
- ❏ Cajun seasoning
- ❏ Garlic powder
- ❏ Bay leaf
- ❏ Dried parsley flakes
- ❏ Dried thyme
- ❏ Ground nutmeg
- ❏ Worcestershire sauce
- ❏ Pasta (bow tie pasta)

Thursday's Dish
Bow Tie Beef Skillet, pg. 29

mon.   tues.   wed.   fri.

Try something different every day...

Familiar recipes take on tempting taste twists with this week's menu planner! New ingredients, surprise seasonings and unexpected flavor combos all pop up in favorite, old-fashioned comfort foods for a week of satisfying options you'll have hot on the table in 30 minutes or less. But be prepared with extra servings because your family will be clamoring for seconds!

Refrigerated tortellini cooks quickly, but you can also use dried tortellini in this pasta, sausage and pepper dish.
—*Taste of Home Test Kitchen*

About Italian Sausage: *(tip)* Italian sausage links come in several varieties, such as mild (a balanced blend of herbs and spices), hot (featuring zesty seasonings such as crushed red pepper flakes) and sweet (with a hint of fresh sweet basil).

30 Roasted Pepper Tortellini

prep/total time: 25 min.

1 package (20 ounces) refrigerated
cheese tortellini
5 Italian sausage links
2 tablespoons olive oil
1 jar (15-1/2 ounces) roasted sweet
red peppers, drained
1 can (15 ounces) pizza sauce
1 cup (4 ounces) shredded
part-skim mozzarella cheese
2 tablespoons shredded Parmesan
cheese

Cook the tortellini according to package directions. Meanwhile, in a large skillet, cook sausage in oil over medium heat until no longer pink; drain. Cut into 1/4-in. slices.

Place the peppers in a blender or food processor; cover and process until smooth. Drain tortellini. Add the tortellini, pureed peppers and pizza sauce to the skillet; stir to combine. Cook for 5 minutes or until heated through. Sprinkle with the mozzarella and Parmesan cheeses; cover and heat until cheese is melted. **Yield:** 6 servings.

This golden fish has a slightly crunchy coating with a nice cornmeal flavor. It's a delicious, easy-to-fix recipe.
—Taste of Home Test Kitchen

(tip) **Better Breading:** To help breading adhere to the fish, pat fillets dry and coat lightly with flour before dipping in egg and dredging in cornmeal coating. Let stand for 5 to 10 minutes before frying.

Strawberry Spinach Salad, pg. 183

Cornmeal-Crusted Catfish **(30)**

prep/total time: 30 min.

1 egg, lightly beaten
2 tablespoons lemon juice
1/2 cup all-purpose flour
1/4 cup yellow cornmeal
1 teaspoon Cajun seasoning
1/2 teaspoon garlic powder
1/2 teaspoon salt
4 catfish fillets (6 ounces *each*)
3 tablespoons vegetable oil

In a shallow bowl, combine the egg and lemon juice. In another shallow bowl, combine the flour, cornmeal, Cajun seasoning, garlic powder and salt. Dip catfish into egg mixture, then coat with cornmeal mixture.

In a large skillet, heat the oil over medium heat. Fry fillets, two at a time, for 5-6 minutes on each side or until fish flakes easily with a fork. **Yield:** 4 servings.

Turkey strips nestled in a quick-to-fix cheese sauce make a delicious weeknight dinner.
—Taste of Home Test Kitchen

- - - - - - - - - - - -

Cooking with White Wine: *(tip)* White wine for cooking should be strong and dry, not sour or fruity. Wine labeled "cooking wine" has an inferior flavor. Instead, a good, dry white vermouth is an excellent choice.

30 Swiss Turkey Tenderloin Strips

prep/total time: 30 min.

1 package (20 ounces) turkey breast tenderloins, cut into thin strips
1/2 teaspoon salt
1/4 teaspoon pepper
3 tablespoons olive oil
1 teaspoon minced garlic
2 tablespoons all-purpose flour
1 cup chicken broth
1/2 cup white wine
3 cups (12 ounces) shredded Swiss cheese
1 package (10 ounces) fresh spinach, trimmed
1/4 cup water

Season turkey with salt and pepper. In a large skillet, saute turkey in oil for 6-8 minutes or until no longer pink. Remove with a slotted spoon and set aside.

In the drippings, saute garlic until tender. Stir in the flour, broth and wine until blended. Bring to a boil over medium heat; cook and stir for 1-2 minutes or until thickened. Reduce heat to low. Slowly add cheese; cook and stir for 2 minutes or until cheese is melted and sauce is blended. Add turkey; heat through.

In a large saucepan or Dutch oven, cook spinach in water for 3-5 minutes or until wilted; drain. Serve turkey mixture over spinach. **Yield:** 4 servings.

This one-pot family pleaser is a snap to make. It's tasty, goes together quickly and I'm always asked for the recipe. Nobody can believe it's so simple.
—Tammy Perrault
Lancaster, Ohio

Bow Tie Beef Skillet ⏱30

prep/total time: 25 min.

1 pound ground beef
1/2 teaspoon salt
1/8 teaspoon pepper
2 cups uncooked bow tie pasta
1 can (14-1/2 ounces) diced tomatoes, drained
1-1/3 cups beef broth
1 can (8 ounces) tomato sauce
1 tablespoon Worcestershire sauce
3 medium yellow summer squash, thinly sliced
3/4 cup chopped green pepper
1 cup (4 ounces) shredded Parmesan cheese, *divided*

In a large skillet, cook beef over medium heat until no longer pink; drain. Sprinkle with salt and pepper. Stir in the pasta, tomatoes, broth, tomato sauce and Worcestershire sauce. Bring to a boil. Reduce heat; cover and simmer for 10-12 minutes.

Add squash and green pepper. Cook, uncovered, 3-4 minutes longer or until pasta and vegetables are tender, stirring occasionally. Add 1/2 cup cheese. Cook for 1-2 minutes or until cheese is melted. Sprinkle with remaining cheese. **Yield:** 5 servings.

Homey, from-scratch meals don't have to be a thing of the past, as this speedy recipe proves.
—Taste of Home Test Kitchen

- - - - - - - - - - - -

Chicken Solution: *(tip)* Simmer the chicken breasts you bought this week in the 4 cups broth until the chicken is no longer pink and the juices run clear. Remove, cube and set aside. Add water to the broth if necessary to equal 4 cups and continue with recipe.

Quicker Chicken 'n' Dumplings

prep/total time: 30 min.

4 cups chicken broth
1/2 cup sliced celery
1/2 cup sliced carrots
1 bay leaf
1-1/2 teaspoons dried parsley flakes, *divided*
2 cups biscuit/baking mix
1/4 teaspoon dried thyme
Dash ground nutmeg
2/3 cup milk
3 cups cubed cooked chicken breast

In a 5-qt. Dutch oven or kettle, combine the broth, celery, carrots, bay leaf and 1 teaspoon parsley; bring to a boil.

For dumplings, combine the biscuit mix, thyme and nutmeg in a bowl; stir in milk and remaining parsley just until moistened. Drop by tablespoonfuls onto boiling broth. Cook, uncovered, for 10 minutes; cover and cook 10 minutes longer.

With a slotted spoon, remove dumplings to a serving dish; keep warm. Bring broth to a boil; reduce heat. Add chicken; heat through. Discard the bay leaf. Spoon over dumplings. **Yield:** 4 servings.

week five

5

Monday's Dish
Zesty Grilled Chops, pg. 32

tues.   wed.   thurs.   fri.

shopping list

- ○ 6 boneless skinless chicken breast halves (4 ounces *each*)
- ○ 6 bone-in pork loin chops (8 ounces *each*)
- ○ 1 pound beef flank steak
- ○ 1 package (20 ounces) turkey tenderloins
- ○ 1/2 cup crushed cornflakes
- ○ 1 tablespoon chili sauce
- ○ 1 can (8 ounces) tomato sauce
- ○ 1 package (19 ounces) frozen cheese tortellini
- ○ 1 cup frozen mixed vegetables
- ○ 1 medium sweet red pepper
- ○ 1/4 cup ground walnuts
- ○ 2 tablespoons minced fresh basil
- ○ 1 tablespoon chopped green onion
- ○ 2 medium lemons
- ○ 2 medium green peppers
- ○ 2/3 cup shredded part-skim mozzarella cheese
- ○ 2 cups heavy whipping cream

STAPLES FOR THE WEEK

- ❒ Garlic cloves *or* prepared minced garlic
- ❒ Onion
- ❒ Vegetable oil
- ❒ White wine vinegar
- ❒ Salt
- ❒ White pepper
- ❒ Italian seasoning
- ❒ Garlic powder
- ❒ Dried parsley flakes
- ❒ Ground ginger
- ❒ Flour
- ❒ Grated Parmesan cheese
- ❒ Milk
- ❒ Eggs
- ❒ Butter
- ❒ Soy sauce
- ❒ Brown sugar
- ❒ Sugar
- ❒ Cornstarch
- ❒ Rice
- ❒ Instant *or* prepared, refrigerated mashed potatoes

Entertaining ideas for family and friends!

Unexpected guests or a planned casual dinner? No problem! This week, take your pick from any of these make-it-in-minutes meals so you can enjoy time with your family and friends—and still serve a special entree. Pick a savory side dish or an easy salad from those starting on page 147. If you're entertaining a larger group, round out your menu with an assortment of breads and rolls from the bakery.

My sister gave me the recipe for this easy five-ingredient marinade.
—Bernice Germann
Napoleon, Ohio

- - - - - - - - - - - -

Buy Thicker Chops: *(tip)*

When buying bone-in pork chops, try to find cuts at least 3/4 inch or thicker. The meat closest to the bone takes longer to cook, so thinner chops tend to overcook and dry out before the area close to the bone is cooked.

Zesty Grilled Chops

prep: 5 min. + marinating **grill:** 10 min.

3/4 cup soy sauce
1/4 cup lemon juice
1 tablespoon brown sugar
1 tablespoon chili sauce
1/4 teaspoon garlic powder
6 bone-in pork loin chops
(8 ounces *each*)

In a large resealable plastic bag, combine the soy sauce, lemon juice, brown sugar, chili sauce and garlic powder. Remove 1/4 cup for basting and refrigerate. Add pork chops to the bag; seal bag and turn to coat. Refrigerate for 3 hours or overnight, turning once.

Drain and discard marinade from the pork chops. Grill chops, covered, over medium-hot heat for 4 minutes. Turn; baste with reserved marinade. Grill 4-7 minutes longer or until juices run clear. **Yield:** 6 servings.

This is a shortcut version of a rich, creamy pasta dish I sampled years ago. I've served this tortellini as both a meatless entree and special side dish.
—Mickie Taft
Milwaukee, Wisconsin

(tip) Keeping Basil Fresh: Select fresh basil with evenly colored leaves and no wilting. Refrigerate basil, wrapped in barely damp paper towels, in a plastic bag for up to 4 days.

Pesto Pepper Tortellini (20)

prep/total time: 20 min.

1 package (19 ounces) frozen
  cheese tortellini
1/2 cup julienned sweet red pepper
1-1/2 teaspoons minced garlic
2 tablespoons butter
2 cups heavy whipping cream
1/4 cup ground walnuts
2 tablespoons minced fresh basil
1 tablespoon chopped green onion

Cook tortellini according to package directions. Meanwhile, in a large skillet, saute red pepper and garlic in butter until pepper is crisp-tender. Stir in cream; cook for 8-10 minutes or until slightly thickened. Add the walnuts, basil and onion; heat through. Drain tortellini; add to sauce and toss to coat.
Yield: 4 servings.

You can use any leftover fresh vegetables you have on hand in this quick dish.
—Taste of Home Test Kitchen

Prep Pointers: *(tip)* Get a start on this dinner by stopping at the deli counter to pick up the mashed potatoes. Or use instant or prepared, refrigerated mashed potatoes. For the cubed cooked turkey, cook the turkey tenderloins you bought this week as directed in the tip on page 17.

⓴ Creamed Turkey On Mashed Potatoes

prep/total time: 20 min.

1/2 cup chopped onion
2 tablespoons butter
2 tablespoons all-purpose flour
1/4 teaspoon salt
1/8 teaspoon white pepper
2 cups milk
2 cups cubed cooked turkey breast
1 cup frozen mixed vegetables
2 cups hot mashed potatoes

In a large saucepan, saute the onion in butter until tender. Sprinkle with flour, salt and pepper. Stir in the milk until blended.

Bring to a boil; cook and stir for 2 minutes or until thickened and bubbly. Add the turkey and vegetables; cover and simmer until heated through. Serve over mashed potatoes. **Yield:** 4 servings.

This wonderfully tender steak is a treat. When my mother-in-law shared the recipe, she said it cooks up in no time...and she was right.
—Susan Adair
Muncie, Indiana

(tip) **Storing Vinegar:** Red and white wine vinegars are pleasantly pungent. All vinegars should be stored airtight in a cool, dark place. Unopened, they will keep indefinitely. Once opened, they can be stored for about 6 months.

Gingered Pepper Steak ㉚

prep/total time: 25 min.

2 teaspoons sugar
2 teaspoons cornstarch
1/4 teaspoon ground ginger
1/4 cup reduced-sodium soy sauce
1 tablespoon white wine vinegar
1 pound beef flank steak, thinly sliced
2 medium green peppers, julienned
1 teaspoon vegetable oil
Hot cooked rice, optional

In a large bowl, combine the sugar, cornstarch, ginger, soy sauce and vinegar until smooth. Add beef and toss to coat; set aside.

In a large skillet or wok, stir-fry the green peppers in oil until crisp-tender, about 3 minutes. Remove with a slotted spoon and keep warm. Add the beef with marinade to pan; stir-fry for 3 minutes or until meat reaches desired doneness. Return peppers to pan; heat through. Serve over rice if desired. **Yield:** 4 servings.

I make this moist chicken often in summer when we want something quick and yummy. With its golden coating, this entree is special enough for company.
—Roni Goodell
Spanish Fork, Utah

Time-Saving Strategy: *(tip)*
Keep a box of cornflake crumbs in your cupboard for a quick chicken coating. You can find boxes of crushed cornflakes in your supermarket near the bread crumbs.

30 Chicken Breast Cacciatore

prep/total time: 30 min.

1 can (8 ounces) tomato sauce
1 teaspoon Italian seasoning
1/4 teaspoon garlic powder
1/2 cup crushed cornflakes
1/4 cup grated Parmesan cheese
1 teaspoon dried parsley flakes
1 egg
6 boneless skinless chicken breast halves (4 ounces *each*)
2/3 cup shredded part-skim mozzarella cheese

In a microwave-safe bowl, combine the tomato sauce, Italian seasoning and garlic powder. Cover and microwave on high for 1-1/2 minutes; stir. Cook at 50% power for 2-4 minutes or until mixture simmers, stirring once; set aside.

In a shallow bowl, combine the cornflakes, Parmesan cheese and parsley. In another shallow bowl, beat the egg. Dip chicken into egg, then roll in cornflake mixture. Place in a lightly greased shallow 3-qt. microwave-safe dish.

Cover and microwave on high for 8 to 9-1/2 minutes, rotating a half turn after 4 minutes. Pour tomato mixture over chicken; sprinkle with mozzarella cheese. Cook, uncovered, at 50% power for 2-4 minutes or until chicken juices run clear. **Yield:** 6 servings.

Friday's Dish
Turkey Tenderloin
Supreme, pg. 42

mon   tues   wed.   thurs

shopping list

- 1 pound boneless beef sirloin steak
- 1 package (20 ounces) turkey breast tenderloins
- 1 pound boneless skinless chicken breasts
- 1/2 pound sliced bacon
- 3 medium potatoes
- 1/3 cup chopped green onions
- 5 medium carrots
- 1/2 cup sliced fresh mushrooms
- Sweet red pepper
- 3 tablespoons minced fresh parsley
- 1-1/2 teaspoons minced fresh rosemary
- 1 package (6.2 ounces) fast-cooking long grain and wild rice mix
- 6 hamburger buns
- 1 can (10-3/4 ounces) condensed cream of potato soup
- 1 can (10-3/4 ounces) condensed cream of chicken soup
- 8 ounces process cheese (Velveeta)
- 2 packages (11.4 ounces *each*) frozen crunchy breaded fish fillets
- 1 teaspoon horseradish sauce
- 1-1/2 cups deli coleslaw

STAPLES FOR THE WEEK

- Onion
- Olive oil
- Salt
- Garlic-pepper seasoning blend
- Milk
- Butter
- Mayonnaise
- Ketchup
- Stone-ground mustard
- Hot pepper sauce
- Chicken broth (three 14-1/2 ounce cans) *or* chicken bouillon
- Rice (long grain)

Weekend planning cuts weekday prep...

Take a few extra minutes during a Sunday afternoon to get your kitchen prep work out of the way for the week! When you return from the grocery store, gather your fresh vegetables, such as onions, carrots, mushrooms and peppers, then slice and dice according to this week's menu. Store your chopped veggies in plastic containers or storage bags in the fridge until you're ready to add them to your recipes.

While this colorful stovetop supper is perfect for everyday family meals, it also makes a lovely company dinner.
—Frances Musser
Newmanstown,
Pennsylvania

Storing Rice: *(tip)*
Store uncooked white rice in an airtight container in a cool, dark place for up to 2 years. Brown rice should be used within 6 months.

Carrot Chicken Pilaf

prep: 20 min. **cook:** 20 min. + standing

1	**pound boneless skinless chicken breasts, cut into thin strips**
1/4	**cup butter**
1-1/2	**cups uncooked long grain rice**
5	**medium carrots, sliced**
1	**medium onion, chopped**
1/2	**cup sliced fresh mushrooms**
1/4	**cup chopped sweet red pepper**
4	**cups chicken broth**
2	**tablespoons minced fresh parsley**

In a large skillet, brown chicken in butter. Remove and keep warm. Add the rice, carrots, onion, mushrooms and red pepper to the skillet. Cook and stir until rice is browned and onion is tender.

Stir in broth. Place chicken over rice mixture. Bring to a boil. Reduce heat; cover and simmer for 20-25 minutes or until rice is tender. Stir in parsley. Let stand for 5 minutes before serving. **Yield:** 6 servings.

Unpeeled potato slices, which are precooked in the microwave, speed up the cooking time for this meal. Fresh rosemary adds a nice flavor to the skillet dish.
—Taste of Home Test Kitchen

(tip) Don't Peel Potatoes: To decrease the prep time, don't peel the potatoes. You can also cook them ahead of time and refrigerate until ready to use.

Skillet Beef and Potatoes 30

prep/total time: 25 min.

3	medium potatoes, halved and cut into 1/4-inch slices
1/3	cup water
1/2	teaspoon salt
1	pound boneless beef sirloin steak, cut into thin strips
2	teaspoons garlic-pepper seasoning blend
1/2	cup chopped onion
3	tablespoons olive oil, *divided*
1-1/2	teaspoons minced fresh rosemary

Place potatoes, water and salt in a microwave-safe dish. Cover and microwave on high for 6-10 minutes or until tender; drain. Season beef with pepper blend. In a large skillet, stir-fry beef and onion in 2 tablespoons oil for 5 minutes or until beef is no longer pink.

Meanwhile, in another skillet, stir-fry potatoes in remaining oil for 5 minutes or until browned. Stir in beef mixture. Sprinkle with rosemary. **Yield:** 4 servings.

We often eat soups when there's not a lot of time to cook. I replaced the wild rice requested in the original recipe with a boxed rice mix. This creamy concoction is now a family favorite.
—Lisa Hofer
Hitchcock,
South Dakota

30 Cheesy Wild Rice Soup

prep/total time: 25 min.

- 1 package (6.2 ounces) fast-cooking long grain and wild rice mix
- 4 cups milk
- 1 can (10-3/4 ounces) condensed cream of potato soup, undiluted
- 8 ounces process cheese (Velveeta), cubed
- 1/2 pound sliced bacon, cooked and crumbled

In a large saucepan, prepare rice according to package directions. Stir in the milk, soup and cheese. Cook and stir until cheese is melted. Garnish with bacon. **Yield:** 8 servings.

Soup & Salad Supper

Complement steaming bowls of soup with a cool, crisp side salad. Supermarkets offer a variety of salad mixes with dressings like Caesar, Romano and ranch. Embellish them by tossing in a variety of your favorite fresh vegetables. Any leftover salad should be eaten within 2 days and before the "Best If Used By" date on the package.

Although we used a garlic-and-herb variety of frozen fish to make these sandwiches, feel free to use your favorite flavor. Ideas include lemon-pepper, ranch or Parmesan.
—Taste of Home Test Kitchen

(tip) Eat Your Veggies: In place of french fries, serve carrot and celery sticks as a healthy side. To keep some handy, clean and slice carrots and celery. Store them in a covered container in the refrigerator crisper for up to 2 weeks.

Fish Po'Boys (30)

prep/total time: 30 min.

2	packages (11.4 ounces *each*) frozen crunchy breaded fish fillets
1/2	cup mayonnaise
1	tablespoon minced fresh parsley
1	tablespoon ketchup
2	teaspoons stone-ground mustard
1	teaspoon horseradish sauce
2 to 4	drops hot pepper sauce
1-1/2	cups deli coleslaw
6	hamburger buns, split

Bake fish according to package directions. Meanwhile, in a small bowl, combine the mayonnaise, parsley, ketchup, mustard, horseradish sauce and hot pepper sauce until blended. Spoon 1/4 cup coleslaw onto the bottom of each bun; top with two pieces of fish. Spread with sauce; replace bun tops. **Yield:** 6 servings.

We're a busy hockey and figure skating family, so we're always on the go. Served over rice, this fast skillet supper makes a good home-cooked meal when there's little time.
—Nancy Levin
Chesterfield,
Missouri

Turkey Tenderloin Supreme

prep/total time: 20 min.

1 package (20 ounces) turkey breast tenderloins, cut into 1-inch slices
1 tablespoon butter
1/3 cup chopped green onions
1 can (10-3/4 ounces) condensed cream of chicken soup, undiluted
1/4 cup water

In a large skillet, brown the turkey in butter. Add onions; cook for 1-2 minutes. Combine the soup and water; pour over turkey. Bring to a boil. Reduce heat; cover and simmer for 8-10 minutes or until meat juices run clear. **Yield:** 4 servings.

shopping list

- ◯ 1 head green leaf lettuce
- ◯ 3 large tomatoes
- ◯ 2 packages (.75 ounce *each*) fresh basil
- ◯ 2 pounds boneless skinless chicken breasts
- ◯ 1 pound ground beef
- ◯ 4 salmon fillets (6 ounces *each*, 1-1/2 pounds total)
- ◯ 4 boneless beef sirloin steaks (6 ounces *each*, 1-1/2 pounds total)
- ◯ 1 package (8 ounces) shredded part-skim mozzarella cheese
- ◯ 1 package (5 ounces) shredded Parmesan cheese
- ◯ 1 package (12 ounces) pita breads
- ◯ 1 Italian bread shell crust (14 ounces)
- ◯ 1 package (25 ounces) nacho cheese tortilla chips
- ◯ 1 jar (16 ounces) Catalina dressing
- ◯ 1 can (15 ounces) black beans

Thursday's Dish
Dressed-Up Steaks, pg. 47

mon *tues* *wed* *fri*

STAPLES FOR THE WEEK

- ☐ Olive oil
- ☐ Minced garlic
- ☐ Lemon juice
- ☐ Mayonnaise
- ☐ Eggs
- ☐ Dried oregano
- ☐ Salt
- ☐ Pepper

Appetizing entrees appeal to everyone...

Grown-ups at the table will swoon over the succulent selections on this week's menu—great choices to serve when introducing young diners to new flavors. But children and kids at heart alike will love the fast, flavorful finger foods. Round out any of these entrees with servings of chilled fresh fruits. It's a great way to sneak in nourishing nutrients and satisfy after-dinner sweet tooths.

After assembling this mild main-dish salad, be sure to set aside the remaining canned black beans to use in Wednesday's meal.
—Taste of Home Test Kitchen

Prep Work: **(tip)** Clean the entire head of green leaf lettuce tonight to ease dinner prep later in the week. Set aside eight leaves for Friday's sandwiches and tear up the rest.

⏲ 20 Black Bean Taco Salad
prep/total time: 20 min.

1 pound ground beef
4 cups torn leaf lettuce
1 large tomato, chopped
1 cup canned black beans, rinsed and drained
1/2 cup Catalina salad dressing
4 cups nacho cheese tortilla chips

In a large skillet, cook beef over medium heat until no longer pink; drain. In a large bowl, combine the lettuce, tomato, beans and beef. Drizzle with dressing and toss to coat. Arrange tortilla chips on a serving plate; top with beef mixture. **Yield:** 4 servings.

Homemade pesto adds instant flair to these simple salmon fillets that bake in the oven.
—Taste of Home Test Kitchen

- - - - - - - - - - - -

(tip) **Head Start:** This recipe gives you a head start on tomorrow night's dinner, because it makes enough extra pesto for the Chicken Pizza.

Catalina Parmesan Salad, pg. 175

Basil Salmon
prep: 15 min. **bake:** 25 min.

1-1/2 cups fresh basil leaves
3 tablespoons plus 2 teaspoons olive oil
1-1/2 teaspoons minced garlic
3/4 teaspoon pepper
1/2 teaspoon lemon juice
1/4 teaspoon salt
1 tablespoon plus 4 teaspoons shredded Parmesan cheese, *divided*
4 salmon fillets (6 ounces *each*)

For pesto, combine basil, oil, garlic, pepper, lemon juice, salt and 1 tablespoon Parmesan cheese in a food processor; cover and process until finely chopped. Place the salmon in a greased 13-in. x 9-in. x 2-in. baking dish. Spread 2 tablespoons of pesto over fillets. (Cover and refrigerate remaining pesto for tomorrow's Chicken Pizza or another use.)

Bake, uncovered, at 400° for 20-22 minutes or until fish flakes easily with a fork. Sprinkle with remaining cheese. Bake 2-3 minutes longer or until cheese is melted. **Yield:** 4 servings.

Your family will never guess that this fun twist on typical pizza uses up leftover pesto. Loaded with chicken and black beans, hearty slices will fill them up fast.
—*Taste of Home Test Kitchen*

- - - - - - - - - - - -

Quick Change:  **tip** Next time you make this pizza, hurry it along even more by using rotisserie chicken from the deli and prepared pesto from a jar.

30 Chicken Pizza

prep/total time: 30 min.

1 **pound boneless skinless chicken breasts, cut into 1-inch strips**
1 **tablespoon olive oil**
1 **prebaked Italian bread shell crust (14 ounces)**
1/4 **cup prepared pesto**
1 **large tomato, chopped**
1/2 **cup canned black beans, rinsed and drained**
1 **cup (4 ounces) shredded part-skim mozzarella cheese**
1/2 **cup shredded Parmesan cheese**

In a large skillet, cook chicken in oil over medium heat for 10-15 minutes or until juices run clear. Place the crust on a lightly greased 12-in. pizza pan. Spread with pesto; top with the chicken, tomato, beans and cheeses. Bake at 400° for 10-12 minutes or until cheese is melted. **Yield:** 6 servings.

A few pantry ingredients nicely season these broiled steaks that are accented with extra Catalina salad dressing.
—*Taste of Home Test Kitchen*

(tip) Fire Up The Grill:
If the weather allows, cook these steaks on your backyard grill for even more flavor.

Two-Cheese Baked Potatoes, pg. 185

Dressed-Up Steaks ⏱20

prep/total time: 20 min.

1 tablespoon olive oil
1-1/2 teaspoons minced garlic
1 teaspoon dried oregano
1 teaspoon pepper
4 boneless beef sirloin steaks
  (6 ounces *each*)
3/4 cup Catalina salad dressing,
  divided

In a small bowl, combine the oil, garlic, oregano and pepper. Rub over both sides of steaks. Brush with 1/4 cup salad dressing. Place on a broiler pan.

Broil 4 in. from the heat for 5-6 minutes on each side or until meat reaches desired doneness (for medium-rare, a meat thermometer should read 145°; medium, 160°; well-done, 170°). Serve with the remaining dressing. **Yield:** 4 servings.

Crushed nacho tortilla chips left over from the taco salad made earlier in the week coat the tender chicken strips in these sandwiches.
—*Taste of Home Test Kitchen*

Preparation Pointers: **tip**
If you prefer, heat each sandwich briefly to melt the cheese before serving. For extra nutrition, substitute whole wheat pitas.

Nacho Chicken Pitas

prep: 20 min. **bake:** 20 min.

1 egg
1 cup crushed nacho cheese tortilla chips
1 pound boneless skinless chicken breasts, cut into 1-inch strips
1/2 cup mayonnaise
4 pita breads (6 inches), halved
8 lettuce leaves
1 large tomato, sliced
1/2 cup shredded part-skim mozzarella cheese

In a shallow bowl, beat the egg. Place crushed chips in another shallow bowl. Dip chicken in egg, then coat with chips. Place in a single layer in a greased 11-in. x 7-in. x 2-in. baking dish. Bake at 400° for 20-25 minutes or until juices run clear.

Spread mayonnaise inside pita halves; line with lettuce. Fill with chicken and tomato; sprinkle with cheese. **Yield:** 4 servings.

shopping list

- ○ 1/2 pound fresh asparagus
- ○ 1/2 pound fresh broccoli
- ○ 2 medium tomatoes
- ○ 2-1/2 pounds boneless skinless chicken breasts
- ○ 1 pound medium shrimp, peeled and deveined
- ○ 4 bone-in pork loin chops (7 ounces *each*, 1-3/4 pounds total)
- ○ 2 packages (17 ounces *each*) refrigerated beef tips with gravy
- ○ 1 package (24 ounces) refrigerated mashed potatoes
- ○ 2 packages (15 ounces *each*) refrigerated pie pastry
- ○ 1 package (8 ounces) shredded cheddar cheese
- ○ 1 package (12.7 to 14.8 ounces) sun-dried tomato tortillas
- ○ 1 bottle (1 pint) orange juice
- ○ 1 pound prepared deli coleslaw
- ○ 1 package (8 ounces) Caribbean rice mix
- ○ 1 can (20 ounces) pineapple tidbits

Wednesday's Dish
Chicken Wellington, pg. 52

mon   tues.   thurs   fri

STAPLES FOR THE WEEK

- ❒ All-purpose flour
- ❒ Butter
- ❒ 1 egg
- ❒ White wine
- ❒ Olive oil
- ❒ Cornstarch
- ❒ Chicken bouillon granules
- ❒ Dried rosemary
- ❒ Rubbed sage
- ❒ Ground ginger
- ❒ Salt
- ❒ Pepper

Get through the market in record time!

With your weekly grocery list in hand, plan your shopping trip according to the layout of your local favorite market. Grab any packaged or boxed non-refrigerated items first, then stop in the produce, meat and refrigerated sections to pick up perishable ones. With good timing, you'll net all the basics you need for a full week of classic tastes like these in less than 30 minutes.

A flavorful rice mix gives a jump start to this skillet supper that's hearty with fresh shrimp, asparagus and tomato. It's colorful and not too spicy, so it will please the whole family.
—Taste of Home
Test Kitchen

🕐30 Caribbean Rice 'n' Shrimp

prep/total time: 25 min.

- 1 package (8 ounces) Caribbean rice mix
- 6 cups water
- 1/2 pound fresh asparagus, trimmed and cut into 1-inch pieces
- 1 pound uncooked medium shrimp, peeled and deveined
- 1 medium tomato, chopped

Prepare rice mix according to package directions, omitting chicken. Meanwhile, in a large saucepan, bring water to a boil. Add asparagus; cover and cook for 2 minutes. Stir in shrimp; cook for 2-3 minutes or until shrimp turn pink. Drain. Add asparagus, shrimp and tomato to rice; toss gently. **Yield:** 4 servings.

Dressing up store-bought convenience items makes this satisfying supper a snap to put on the table. It's hot, hearty and ready to eat in minutes.
—Taste of Home Test Kitchen

Beef Tips on Potatoes (20)

prep/total time: 15 min.

2 packages (17 ounces *each*) refrigerated beef tips with gravy
1 package (24 ounces) refrigerated mashed potatoes
3/4 cup fresh broccoli florets, finely chopped
1 tablespoon water
3/4 cup shredded cheddar cheese, *divided*

Prepare the beef tips and mashed potatoes according to package directions. Place broccoli and water in a microwave-safe dish; cover and microwave on high for 3 minutes or until crisp-tender. Stir the broccoli and 1/2 cup cheese into potatoes. Serve beef tips over potatoes; sprinkle with remaining cheese. **Yield:** 4 servings.

Editor's Note: This recipe was tested in a 1,100-watt microwave.

For an elegant entree, serve this tender chicken tucked inside a golden pie crust and topped with wine sauce.
—*Taste of Home Test Kitchen*

Sauce Stir-In: (tip)
A dry white wine like chardonnay adds an elegant touch to the sauce that tops this special entree. If you don't have any wine on hand, simply eliminate it and prepare the gravy as directed.

Chicken Wellington

prep: 30 min. **bake:** 20 min. + standing

     4 boneless skinless chicken breast
       halves (6 ounces *each*)
     1 tablespoon olive oil
     4 tablespoons butter, softened, *divided*
     1 teaspoon dried rosemary, crushed
   1/2 teaspoon rubbed sage
   1/4 teaspoon *each* salt and pepper
     2 packages (15 ounces *each*)
       refrigerated pie pastry
     1 egg, lightly beaten
1-1/4 teaspoons chicken bouillon granules
1-1/4 cups hot water
     3 tablespoons all-purpose flour
     2 tablespoons white wine

Flatten chicken to 1/4 in. In a skillet, cook chicken in oil and 1 tablespoon butter 4-5 minutes on each side until juices run clear.

Meanwhile, combine rosemary, sage, salt, pepper and 1 tablespoon butter. Unroll pastry sheets; cut each into a 9-in. square (discard scraps). Place a chicken breast half on each square; spread chicken with butter mixture. Fold pastry over chicken. Trim off excess pastry; pinch seams to seal. Place on a greased baking sheet; brush with egg. Bake at 450° for 18-20 minutes or until golden brown. Let stand 10 minutes before serving.

Meanwhile, dissolve bouillon in hot water. In a saucepan, melt remaining butter; stir in flour until smooth. Gradually stir in bouillon and wine. Bring to a boil; cook and stir for 2 minutes or until thickened. Serve with chicken. **Yield:** 4 servings.

Pork chops pick up plenty of sweet flavor when simmered in a ginger-seasoned pineapple mixture.
—Taste of Home Test Kitchen

- - - - - - - - - - - - -

(tip) Pineapple Tidbit: This pork chop recipe leaves you with extra pineapple tidbits. Store them in an airtight container in the fridge to use in Friday's Chicken Coleslaw Wraps.

Balsamic Asparagus, pg. 163

Pineapple Ginger Chops ⊘30

prep/total time: 30 min.

1 can (20 ounces) unsweetened pineapple tidbits
1 teaspoon pepper
1/2 teaspoon ground ginger
4 bone-in pork loin chops (7 ounces *each*)
1 tablespoon butter
1/2 cup orange juice
1 tablespoon cornstarch
1/8 teaspoon salt
1/4 cup water

Drain pineapple, reserving 1/4 cup juice; set aside. Combine pepper and ginger; rub over both sides of pork chops. In a skillet, brown chops in butter for 2-3 minutes on each side. Add the orange juice, 1 cup pineapple and reserved pineapple juice. (Refrigerate remaining pineapple for another use.)

Bring to a boil. Reduce heat; cover and simmer for 15-20 minutes or until meat is tender. Remove pork chops and keep warm. In a small bowl, combine the cornstarch, salt and water until smooth; stir into pan juices. Bring to a boil; cook and stir for 2 minutes or until thickened. Serve with pork. **Yield:** 4 servings.

Leftover pineapple is stirred into deli coleslaw to add refreshing flair to these tasty chicken sandwiches that are rolled in tortillas.
—Taste of Home Test Kitchen

- - - - - - - - - - - - -

Convenient Chicken Strips: **(tip)**

Trim time from meal prep by buying grilled chicken strips rather than cooking fresh chicken yourself.

20 Chicken Coleslaw Wraps

prep/total time: 20 min.

1 **pound boneless skinless chicken breasts, cut into 1-inch strips**
1/4 **teaspoon salt**
1/8 **teaspoon pepper**
1 **tablespoon olive oil**
1-1/2 **cups deli coleslaw**
1/2 **cup pineapple tidbits**
4 **sun-dried tomato tortillas (10 inches), warmed**
1 **medium tomato, sliced**
1 **cup (4 ounces) shredded cheddar cheese**

Sprinkle chicken with salt and pepper. In a skillet, cook chicken in oil over medium heat for 10-15 minutes or until juices run clear. Combine coleslaw and pineapple; spread evenly over each tortilla. Layer with tomato, cheese and chicken; roll up tightly. **Yield:** 4 servings.

Friday's Dish
Smoked Sausage with
Vegetables, pg. 60

shopping list

- ○ 2 packages (9-3/4 ounces *each*) Asian crunch salad mix
- ○ 1 package (6 ounces) fresh baby spinach
- ○ 1 onion
- ○ 1 pork tenderloin (1 pound)
- ○ 1 beef flank steak (1 pound)
- ○ 1 pound smoked sausage
- ○ 1 pound thinly sliced deli turkey
- ○ 1 pound deli pasta salad
- ○ 4 slices provolone cheese
- ○ 2 packages (5.8 ounces *each*) roasted garlic and olive oil couscous
- ○ 1 can (15 ounces) apricot halves
- ○ 1 jar (7 ounces) roasted sweet red peppers
- ○ 1 bottle (8 ounces) Italian salad dressing
- ○ 2 packages (7.6 ounces *each*) frozen Cajun blackened grilled fish fillets
- ○ 1 package (19 ounces) frozen garden vegetable medley
- ○ 1 loaf (10 ounces) frozen garlic bread

STAPLES FOR THE WEEK

- ❑ Olive oil
- ❑ Canola oil
- ❑ Brown sugar
- ❑ Minced garlic
- ❑ Ketchup
- ❑ Cider vinegar
- ❑ Soy sauce
- ❑ Worcestershire sauce
- ❑ Hot pepper sauce
- ❑ Sugar
- ❑ Honey
- ❑ Grated Parmesan cheese
- ❑ Italian seasoning
- ❑ Salt
- ❑ Pepper
- ❑ Ground ginger
- ❑ Ground mustard
- ❑ Paprika

Turn every day into YUMM day...

No matter how hectic your week, you'll find a dinner you can dash to the table with this tasty 5-day planner. Trim even more time by marinating meats the night before, substituting packaged spice mixes for individual seasonings or using leftover steamed veggies instead of opening a new package of frozen ones. Cutting back on time doesn't mean skimping on flavor!

A homemade marinade adds delicious flavor to the stir-fried pork in this salad.
—*Taste of Home Test Kitchen*

Where to Buy the Bagged Salad: *(tip)*
Look for Asian crunch salad mix in the produce section. If you can't find it, pick up mixed greens, snow peas, shredded carrots, chow mein noodles and a bottle of sesame ginger or Asian-style dressing.

Asian Pork Tenderloin Salad

prep: 10 min. + marinating   cook: 5 min.

1 can (15 ounces) apricot halves
1/4 cup soy sauce
1 tablespoon brown sugar
1 tablespoon canola oil
1/2 teaspoon ground ginger
1/2 teaspoon minced garlic
1/4 teaspoon ground mustard
1 pork tenderloin (1 pound), thinly sliced
2 packages (9-3/4 ounces *each*) Asian crunch salad mix

Drain apricots, reserving 1/2 cup juice; set apricots aside. In a large resealable plastic bag, combine the soy sauce, brown sugar, oil, ginger, garlic, mustard and reserved apricot juice; add pork. Seal bag and turn to coat; refrigerate for at least 1 hour.

Drain and discard marinade. In a large skillet or wok, stir-fry pork for 4-5 minutes or until juices run clear. Prepare salad mixes according to package directions; top with apricots and pork. **Yield:** 4 servings.

These warm, open-faced sandwiches make a quick and filling entree. Starting with garlic bread from the frozen food section hurries along the preparation.
—Taste of Home Test Kitchen

(tip) **Put Aside the Peppers:** The sandwiches call for part of a jar of roasted sweet red peppers. Save the remainder to use in tomorrow's menu.

Provolone Turkey Sandwiches 20

prep/total time: 20 min.

1 loaf (10 ounces) frozen garlic bread, thawed
1 pound thinly sliced deli turkey
1 cup fresh baby spinach
1/2 cup roasted sweet red peppers, drained and patted dry
4 slices provolone cheese

Bake garlic bread according to package directions. Layer with turkey, spinach, red peppers and cheese. Bake 3-4 minutes longer or until cheese is melted. Cut into serving-size pieces.
Yield: 4 servings.

It takes just minutes to broil this nicely seasoned flank steak that's served with made-in-minutes couscous. Slicing the meat on an angle across the grain produces the most tender results.
—Taste of Home Test Kitchen

Simple Swap: If you prefer, a pound of sirloin steak can be used instead of the flank steak in this recipe. **(tip)**

⏱30 Flank Steak with Couscous

prep/total time: 25 min.

1 teaspoon olive oil
1 teaspoon minced garlic
1/2 teaspoon Italian seasoning
1/4 teaspoon pepper
1/8 teaspoon salt
1 beef flank steak (1 pound)
2 packages (5.8 ounces *each*) roasted garlic and olive oil couscous
3/4 cup diced roasted sweet red peppers, drained
1/2 cup Italian salad dressing

In a small bowl, combine the first five ingredients; rub over flank steak. Place on a broiler pan. Broil 4 in. from the heat for 7-8 minutes on each side or until the meat reaches desired doneness (for medium-rare, a meat thermometer should read 145°; medium, 160°; well-done, 170°).

Meanwhile, cook couscous according to package directions. Stir in roasted peppers. Thinly slice steak across the grain; drizzle with Italian dressing. Serve with couscous. **Yield:** 4 servings.

A handful of convenience items, including pasta salad from the deli and Cajun-style fish fillets from the freezer section, makes it a snap to put together this super-fast main dish.
—Taste of Home Test Kitchen

Strawberry Breadstick Rolls, pg. 237

Blackened Fish Salad

prep/total time: 25 min.

2 packages (7.6 ounces *each*) frozen Cajun blackened grilled fish fillets
1 pound deli pasta salad
1 cup fresh baby spinach
2 tablespoons grated Parmesan cheese

Bake the fish fillets according to package directions. Meanwhile, in a large bowl, toss the pasta salad and spinach. Divide among four salad plates. Cut fish into slices; arrange over salad. Sprinkle with Parmesan cheese.
Yield: 4 servings.

Try Other Fish (tip)

We used Gorton's brand blackened grilled fish fillets in this main-dish salad recipe, but choose any grilled fish your family enjoys.

Hearty appetites are sure to be satisfied with this great combo of zippy smoked sausage and colorful vegetables. Using a frozen vegetable medley makes it easy to fix.
—Taste of Home Test Kitchen

- - - - - - - - - - - -

Pick Other Vegetables: *tip* The frozen garden vegetable medley shown here contains snap peas, roasted potatoes, red peppers and garden herbs. Feel free to choose whatever combination you prefer.

Smoked Sausage with Vegetables

prep/total time: 30 min.

1 package (19 ounces) frozen garden vegetable medley
1/3 cup chopped onion
1 tablespoon canola oil
1/2 cup water
1/2 cup ketchup
1/4 cup cider vinegar
1 tablespoon Worcestershire sauce
1 tablespoon honey
1 teaspoon ground mustard
1 teaspoon paprika
1/4 teaspoon salt
1/4 teaspoon sugar
1/8 teaspoon pepper
1/8 teaspoon hot pepper sauce
1 pound smoked sausage, sliced

Cook vegetables according to package directions. Meanwhile, in a large skillet, saute onion in oil until tender. Stir in the next 11 ingredients. Add sausage.

Bring to a boil. Reduce heat; simmer, uncovered, for 10-12 minutes or until sauce is slightly thickened and sausage is heated through, stirring occasionally and turning sausage once. Serve with the vegetable medley. **Yield:** 4 servings.

Monday's Dish
Crab Salad Croissants, pg. 62

shopping list

- ○ 1 head leaf lettuce
- ○ 1 bunch celery
- ○ 1/4 pound fresh green beans
- ○ 1 package (8 ounces) sliced fresh mushrooms
- ○ 1 medium tomato
- ○ 1 medium onion
- ○ 1 pound boneless beef sirloin steak
- ○ 7 boneless skinless chicken breast halves (6 ounces *each*)
- ○ 1 package (8 ounces) imitation crabmeat
- ○ 1 package (16 ounces) hot dogs
- ○ 1 carton (15 ounces) fat-free vegetarian chili
- ○ 1 bottle (18 ounces) barbecue sauce
- ○ 1 jar (12 ounces) apricot preserves
- ○ 1 package (14 ounces) instant rice
- ○ 2 packages (4.3 ounces *each*) Parmesan cheese pasta sauce mix
- ○ 4 croissants
- ○ 4 slices pepper Jack cheese
- ○ 1 package (8 ounces) shredded cheddar cheese
- ○ 1 package (16 ounces) frozen asparagus stir-fry vegetable blend
- ○ 1 package (32 ounces) frozen french-fried potatoes

STAPLES FOR THE WEEK

- ❑ Canola oil
- ❑ Milk
- ❑ Soy sauce
- ❑ Mustard
- ❑ Mayonnaise
- ❑ Cornstarch
- ❑ Crushed red pepper flakes
- ❑ Dill weed
- ❑ Minced garlic
- ❑ Salt
- ❑ Pepper

Beat the clock with these fast fixes...

Work, play, meetings, errands, phone calls...when will you ever find time to make dinner? All you need is 30 minutes or less for each of these family-favorite entrees! In fact, some of these surefire hits can even be made ahead of time or reheated— perfect for the nights when you've got to eat and run, but still want to enjoy a family meal.

Celery and onion add crunch to the dill-seasoned crab salad that's tucked into buttery croissants from your grocer's bakery.
—Taste of Home Test Kitchen

Crab Salad Croissants

prep/total time: 15 min.

1 package (8 ounces) imitation crabmeat, chopped
1/2 cup mayonnaise
1/4 cup chopped celery
2 tablespoons shredded cheddar cheese
1 tablespoon finely chopped onion
1 teaspoon prepared mustard
1/4 teaspoon dill weed
1/8 teaspoon salt
1/8 teaspoon pepper
4 lettuce leaves
4 croissants, split

In a small bowl, combine the first nine ingredients. Serve on lettuce-lined croissants. **Yield:** 4 servings.

*Pepper Jack cheese from the deli and bottled barbecue sauce are all you need to dress up these grilled chicken breasts.
—Taste of Home Test Kitchen*

Barbecue Jack Chicken

prep/total time: 25 min.

4 boneless skinless chicken breast
   halves (6 ounces *each*)
4 slices pepper Jack cheese
1 cup barbecue sauce

Carefully cut a pocket in each chicken breast half. Fill with cheese; secure with metal or soaked wooden skewers. Grill chicken, covered, over medium heat or broil 4 in. from the heat for 6-8 minutes on each side or until juices run clear, basting frequently with barbecue sauce. Remove skewers before serving.
Yield: 4 servings.

Convenient Chicken (tip)

Buying skinned and deboned chicken breasts can cut minutes off cooking time. Save money by buying large packages, then rewrap individually and freeze.

Simple Side Salad, pg. 164

Who needs hot dog buns when you serve these saucy chili dogs over french fries from the freezer section? Folks of all ages will enjoy this hearty combo.
—Taste of Home Test Kitchen

- - - - - - - - - - - - - -

Serve As A Snack: These loaded fries are a filling entree, but you can also serve them as a satisfying snack.

30 Chili Cheese Fries

prep/total time: 30 min.

4 cups frozen french-fried potatoes
1 carton (15 ounces) fat-free vegetarian chili
5 hot dogs, halved lengthwise and sliced
1/2 cup chopped onion
1 cup (4 ounces) shredded cheddar cheese

Prepare fries according to package directions. Meanwhile, in a microwave-safe dish, combine the chili, hot dogs and onion. Cover and microwave on high for 5-6 minutes or until heated through, stirring once. Serve over fries; sprinkle with cheese. **Yield:** 4 servings.

Editor's Note: This recipe was tested in a 1,100-watt microwave.

Pasta mixes simplify assembly of this skillet supper that's loaded with tender chicken.
—Taste of Home Test Kitchen

- - - - - - - - - - - - -

(tip) **Vary the Vegetables:** Make this versatile pasta toss any time by using vegetables you have on hand. Substitute broccoli for the green beans and use canned mushrooms in place of fresh.

Parmesan Chicken Pasta (30)

prep/total time: 25 min.

2 packages (4.3 ounces *each*) Parmesan cheese pasta sauce mix
3 boneless skinless chicken breasts (about 1 pound), cut into strips
1 cup sliced fresh mushrooms
1 cup fresh green beans, cut into 1-inch pieces
2 tablespoons canola oil
1 medium tomato, chopped

Prepare pasta mixes according to package directions. Meanwhile, in a large skillet, cook chicken, mushrooms and beans in oil over medium heat for 10-15 minutes or until chicken juices run clear and vegetables are tender; drain. Add to pasta and sauce. Stir in tomato.
Yield: 4 servings.

Editor's Note: This recipe was tested with Lipton Pasta Sides fettuccine and spinach pasta in a Parmesan cheese sauce mix.

Apricot preserves lend sweetness to this tasty beef stir-fry, while red pepper flakes provide a bit of kick. A frozen vegetable medley shaves minutes off prep time...no chopping necessary!
—Taste of Home Test Kitchen

- - - - - - - - - - - - -

Buy Brown Rice: This **(tip)** stir-fry is served over rice, so the grocery list calls for a package of instant white rice. To boost fiber without adding time, buy instant brown rice instead.

(30) Apricot Beef Stir-Fry

prep/total time: 25 min.

> 1 teaspoon cornstarch
> 1/4 cup cold water
> 1/2 cup apricot preserves
> 2 tablespoons soy sauce
> 1/2 teaspoon minced garlic
> 1/4 teaspoon salt
> 1/4 teaspoon crushed red pepper flakes
> 1 pound boneless beef sirloin steak, thinly sliced
> 1 tablespoon canola oil
> 1 package (16 ounces) frozen asparagus stir-fry vegetable blend
> Hot cooked rice

In a small bowl, whisk cornstarch and cold water until smooth. Stir in the apricot preserves, soy sauce, garlic, salt and pepper flakes; set aside.

In a large skillet or wok, stir-fry beef in oil until no longer pink; remove and keep warm. In the same pan, stir-fry the vegetable blend according to package directions. Return beef to the pan. Stir apricot mixture and add to beef mixture. Cook and stir until slightly thickened. Serve with rice. **Yield:** 4 servings.

week eleven (11)

Thursday's Dish
Pine Nut-Crusted Tilapia, pg. 71

Pine Nut-Crusted Tilapia, pg. 71

shopping list

- ○ 2 medium acorn squash
- ○ 1 medium zucchini
- ○ 2 medium onions
- ○ 1 package (6 ounces) fresh baby spinach
- ○ 1 package (5 ounces) spring mix salad greens
- ○ 1 package (6 ounces) baby portobello mushrooms
- ○ 1 pound boneless beef sirloin steak
- ○ 1 pound boneless skinless chicken breasts
- ○ 4 tilapia fillets (6 ounces *each*)
- ○ 1 pound bulk spicy pork sausage
- ○ 1/2 pound sliced bacon
- ○ 1 package (16 ounces) linguine
- ○ 1 package (9.3 ounces) minestrone soup mix
- ○ 1 bottle (16 ounces) balsamic vinaigrette
- ○ 1 package (6 ounces) dried cranberries
- ○ 1 package (4 ounces) pine nuts
- ○ 1 package (8 ounces) cream cheese
- ○ 1 package (4 ounces) blue cheese
- ○ 1 loaf (1 pound) French bread

STAPLES FOR THE WEEK

- ❏ Milk
- ❏ Olive oil
- ❏ Butter
- ❏ Brown sugar
- ❏ Honey
- ❏ Flour
- ❏ Eggs
- ❏ Lemon juice
- ❏ Minced garlic
- ❏ Grated Parmesan cheese
- ❏ Cayenne pepper
- ❏ Dill weed
- ❏ Dried parsley
- ❏ Ground cinnamon
- ❏ Ground nutmeg
- ❏ Lemon-pepper seasoning
- ❏ Pepper
- ❏ Salt

mon. *tues.* *wed.* *th.*

Picture-perfect portions impress everyone!

Surprise your family with quick-as-a-wink recipes that look like you spent hours preparing them! A sprinkle of parmesan cheese, a shake of special seasoning or a last-minute saucy drizzle are 10-second touches you can easily add to any of these entrees to entice even the pickiest eaters around the table. For extra special occasions, serve your meal restaurant-style, plated and ready to enjoy.

A packaged minestrone soup mix is jazzed up with cubed chicken, fresh zucchini, portobello mushrooms and croutons for this satisfying main course.
—Taste of Home Test Kitchen

Cut Time With Purchased Croutons: *(tip)*
To speed along prep, top steaming bowls of this soup with store-bought salad croutons instead of making homemade croutons.

30 Chicken Minestrone

prep/total time: 30 min.

1 package (9.3 ounces) minestrone soup mix
1 medium zucchini, quartered lengthwise and sliced
1 cup chopped baby portobello mushrooms
1 pound boneless skinless chicken breasts, cubed
1 tablespoon olive oil
1/4 cup butter, melted
1 teaspoon dried parsley flakes
6 slices day-old French bread (1 inch thick), cubed

2 tablespoons grated Parmesan cheese

Prepare soup mix according to package directions, adding the zucchini and mushrooms. Meanwhile, in a large skillet, cook chicken in oil for 10-12 minutes or until juices run clear. Stir into soup.

For croutons, in a large bowl, combine butter and parsley. Add bread cubes and toss to coat. Arrange in a single layer on an ungreased baking sheet. Sprinkle with Parmesan cheese. Bake at 400° for 7-8 minutes or until golden brown, stirring occasionally. Serve with soup. **Yield:** 5 servings.

Acorn squash gets a sweet-and-savory treatment when stuffed with sausage, onion, spinach and cranberries to make this pretty entree.
—Taste of Home Test Kitchen

(tip) **Bread Crumb Basics:** Tear a portion of the loaf of French bread left over from Monday's meal into chunks. Process in a blender or food processor in batches to get the 1-1/2 cups of soft bread crumbs needed for this recipe.

Sausage-Stuffed Acorn Squash **30**

prep/total time: 25 min.

2 medium acorn squash
1 pound bulk spicy pork sausage
1/2 cup chopped onion
1 egg
2 tablespoons milk
1 cup fresh baby spinach, finely chopped
1-1/2 cups soft bread crumbs
1/2 cup dried cranberries

Cut squash in half; remove and discard seeds. Place squash cut side down in a microwave-safe dish. Cover and microwave on high for 10-12 minutes or until tender.

Meanwhile, crumble sausage into a large skillet; add onion. Cook over medium heat until meat is no longer pink; drain. In a large bowl, beat egg and milk; stir in the spinach, bread crumbs, cranberries and sausage.

Turn squash cut side up. Stuff with sausage mixture. Cover and microwave on high for 2-3 minutes or until heated through. **Yield:** 4 servings.

Editor's Note: This recipe was tested in a 1,100-watt microwave.

On a chilly evening, this creamy pasta toss is sure to please. It's rich and flavorful with smoky bacon, fresh spinach and toasted pine nuts.
—*Taste of Home Test Kitchen*

Pass Up The Pork: (tip) For a meatless entree, skip the bacon in this pasta dish. Round out the meal with a simple green salad.

(30) Linguine with Garlic Sauce

prep/total time: 30 min.

12 ounces uncooked linguine
1/2 pound sliced bacon, diced
5 cups fresh baby spinach
1/2 cup chopped onion
1/2 teaspoon minced garlic
1-1/4 cups milk
1 package (8 ounces) cream cheese, cubed
2 tablespoons butter
1/2 teaspoon salt
1/4 teaspoon ground nutmeg
1/4 teaspoon pepper
1/2 cup pine nuts, toasted

Cook linguine according to package directions. Meanwhile, in a large skillet, cook bacon over medium heat until crisp. Using a slotted spoon, remove to paper towels; drain, reserving 1 tablespoon drippings.

In the drippings, saute the spinach, onion and garlic until tender. Add the milk, cream cheese, butter, salt, nutmeg and pepper; stir until smooth. Stir in pine nuts and bacon; heat through. Drain pasta; toss with sauce. **Yield:** 4-6 servings.

This golden brown fish is fast to fix and can be served for a special family meal or when you want to impress guests.
—Taste of Home Test Kitchen

(tip) **Grinding Pine Nuts:** To grind pine nuts, pulse them in a food processor just until ground. Do not overprocess, or the nuts will turn into a paste. In a pinch, use walnuts, hazelnuts or pecans instead of pine nuts.

Roasted Italian Vegetables, pg. 191

Pine Nut-Crusted Tilapia 30

prep/total time: 25 min.

1/2 cup pine nuts, ground
1/4 cup all-purpose flour
1/4 teaspoon dill weed
1/4 teaspoon lemon-pepper seasoning
 1 egg
 3 tablespoons lemon juice
 1 teaspoon honey
 4 tilapia fillets (6 ounces *each*)
 2 tablespoons butter
Additional honey, optional

In a shallow bowl, combine the pine nuts, flour, dill and lemon-pepper. In another shallow bowl, combine the egg, lemon juice and honey. Dip fillets in egg mixture, then coat with nut mixture.

In a large nonstick skillet, cook fillets in butter over medium heat for 4-5 minutes on each side or until fish flakes easily with a fork. Drizzle with additional honey if desired. **Yield:** 4 servings.

Caramelized onion and sirloin steak seasoned with a cinnamon rub make this main-dish salad different from typical versions. It's easy to toss together with packaged greens, blue cheese, dried cranberries and store-bought vinaigrette.
—Taste of Home Test Kitchen

Grill It Instead: (tip) If the weather is conducive to grilling, cook the sirloin on your backyard grill instead of broiling it.

30 Savory Steak Salad

prep/total time: 30 min.

2 tablespoons brown sugar, *divided*
1 teaspoon salt
3/4 teaspoon ground cinnamon
1/4 teaspoon cayenne pepper
1/4 teaspoon pepper
1 boneless beef sirloin steak (1 inch thick and 1 pound)
3/4 cup balsamic vinaigrette, *divided*
1 medium onion, sliced
2 tablespoons butter
1 package (5 ounces) spring mix salad greens
1/2 cup dried cranberries
1/4 cup crumbled blue cheese

In a bowl, combine 1 tablespoon brown sugar, salt, cinnamon, cayenne and pepper. Rub over both sides of steak. Brush with 1/4 cup vinaigrette. Place steak on a broiler pan. Broil 4 in. from heat for 5-6 minutes on each side or until meat reaches desired doneness (for medium-rare, a meat thermometer should read 145°; medium, 160°; well-done, 170°).

In a skillet, saute onion in butter for 10 minutes or until tender. Add remaining brown sugar; cook and stir over medium heat for 5-10 minutes until onion is browned.

Cut steak across the grain into thin slices. Combine the greens, cranberries, blue cheese, onion and beef. Drizzle with remaining vinaigrette; toss to coat. **Yield:** 4 servings.

week twelve

Tuesday's Dish
Swiss Cobb
Salad, pg. 75

shopping list

- ○ 2 bunches green leaf lettuce
- ○ 3 medium tomatoes
- ○ 1/2 pound fresh sugar snap peas
- ○ 1-1/4 pounds sliced deli roast beef
- ○ 1 pound cubed fully cooked ham
- ○ 1 package (2.1 ounces) fully cooked bacon
- ○ 6 boneless skinless chicken breast halves (6 ounces *each*)
- ○ 1 pouch (3.6 ounces) roasted garlic instant mashed potatoes
- ○ 1 jar (12 ounces) honey mustard
- ○ 1 jar (4 ounces) prepared horseradish
- ○ 1 loaf (12 ounces) focaccia bread
- ○ 1 package (2-count) hard-cooked eggs
- ○ 6 ounces deli Swiss cheese
- ○ 1 container (8 ounces) sour cream
- ○ 1 package (16 ounces) frozen corn
- ○ 1 package (24 ounces) frozen pasta, broccoli and Alfredo sauce

STAPLES FOR THE WEEK

- ❒ Olive oil
- ❒ Butter
- ❒ Red wine vinegar
- ❒ Mayonnaise
- ❒ Milk
- ❒ All-purpose flour
- ❒ Sugar
- ❒ Dried basil
- ❒ Dried parsley flakes
- ❒ Dried thyme
- ❒ Dried oregano
- ❒ Pepper
- ❒ Rubbed sage
- ❒ Salt

Solve the "what's for dinner" dilemma...

Not sure if you're in the mood for a salad or a casserole? Something light or a little more substantial? Then feel free to mix up the days of this week's planner! No matter what you're craving, you'll find savory satisfaction with these five selections. Each one partners well with fluffy biscuits, savory muffins or crusty hard rolls from the bakery.

A creamy horseradish spread adds zip to each satisfying wedge of this stacked sandwich. It tastes special, yet is incredibly simple to prepare. Use any bread you like or change the sandwich fillings to suit your tastes.
—Taste of Home Test Kitchen

Save for Tomorrow's Salad: *(tip)*

Use some of the deli roast beef in these sandwiches, and cut the remainder into strips for tomorrow's salad.

⏲ 20 Roast Beef BLT

prep/total time: 15 min.

1 loaf (12 ounces) focaccia bread
1/2 cup mayonnaise
1 teaspoon prepared horseradish
3 lettuce leaves
3/4 pound sliced deli roast beef
6 bacon strips, cooked
8 slices tomato

Cut focaccia bread in half horizontally. Combine mayonnaise and horseradish; spread over cut sides of bread. Layer the lettuce, roast beef, bacon and tomato over bread bottom; replace bread top. Cut into wedges. **Yield:** 4 servings.

Topped with ham, roast beef, bacon and other fixings, this hearty salad has an excellent blend of flavors. A from-scratch vinaigrette adds the refreshing final touch.
—Taste of Home Test Kitchen

(tip) Cook Your Own Eggs: This week's shopping list calls for hard-cooked eggs from the dairy section for this salad. But you can easily cook a few the night before... and save extras for a snack.

Swiss Cobb Salad (20)

prep/total time: 20 min.

8 cups torn leaf lettuce
1/2 pound sliced deli roast beef, cut into strips
1/4 pound cubed fully cooked ham
1 medium tomato, chopped
2 hard-cooked eggs, chopped
4 bacon strips, cooked and crumbled
1/2 cup shredded Swiss cheese

DRESSING:
1/2 cup olive oil
3 tablespoons red wine vinegar
2 tablespoons honey mustard
2 teaspoons sugar
3/4 teaspoon dried oregano
1/8 teaspoon pepper

In a serving bowl, layer the lettuce, roast beef, ham, tomato, eggs, bacon and cheese. In a jar with a tight-fitting lid, combine the dressing ingredients; shake well. Serve with the salad. **Yield:** 4 servings.

It's easy to treat your family to this mashed-potato-topped casserole featuring tender chicken, sugar snap peas and sweet corn in a homemade cheese sauce.
—Taste of Home Test Kitchen

- - - - - - - - - - - - -

Finishing Fast Touch: **(tip)** For a pretty, golden top, assemble the shepherd's pie in an ovenproof skillet and bake as directed, then broil for 5 minutes.

Chicken Shepherd's Pie

prep: 25 min. **bake:** 25 min.

2 boneless skinless chicken breast halves (6 ounces *each*), cubed
4 tablespoons butter, *divided*
1 pouch (3.6 ounces) roasted garlic mashed potatoes
3 tablespoons all-purpose flour
2-1/4 cups milk
1 teaspoon rubbed sage
1 teaspoon dried thyme
1/2 teaspoon *each* salt and pepper
1 cup (4 ounces) shredded Swiss cheese, *divided*
1 cup fresh sugar snap peas, trimmed and chopped
1/2 cup frozen corn

In a small skillet, cook chicken in 1 tablespoon butter until no longer pink; set aside and keep warm. Prepare mashed potatoes according to package directions.

Meanwhile, in a large saucepan, melt remaining butter over medium heat. Whisk in flour until smooth. Gradually add milk; stir in seasonings. Bring to a boil. Reduce heat; cook and stir for 1-2 minutes or thickened. Remove from the heat. Stir in 3/4 cup Swiss cheese until melted. Add peas, corn and chicken. Transfer to a greased 2-qt. baking dish. Top with mashed potatoes; sprinkle with remaining cheese.

Bake, uncovered, at 350° for 25-30 minutes or until heated through. Let stand for 5 minutes before serving. **Yield:** 6 servings.

A rich gravy made with honey mustard and sour cream drapes nicely over these golden brown chicken breasts.
—Taste of Home Test Kitchen

(tip) Flattening Chicken Breasts: You can flatten the chicken breasts to shave minutes off cooking time, but you'll need a very large skillet to cook all four at once.

Chicken with Mustard Gravy (30)

prep/total time: 25 min.

4 boneless skinless chicken breast halves (6 ounces *each*)
1/2 teaspoon salt, *divided*
1/4 teaspoon pepper, *divided*
2 tablespoons butter
4 teaspoons honey mustard
1 tablespoon milk
1/2 teaspoon dried basil
1/2 teaspoon dried parsley flakes
1/2 cup sour cream

Rub chicken with 1/4 teaspoon salt and 1/8 teaspoon pepper. In a large skillet over medium heat, cook chicken in butter for 6-8 minutes on each side or until no longer pink. Remove and keep warm.

In the same skillet, combine the mustard, milk, basil, parsley, and remaining salt and pepper. Cook and stir over low heat until heated through. Remove from the heat; stir in sour cream. Serve with chicken. **Yield:** 4 servings.

This fuss-free entree comes together in a jiffy with help from a frozen pasta and veggie combo. Adding ham and fresh sugar snap peas really jazzes it up. Stir some red pepper flakes into the creamy mixture for an extra kick.
—Taste of Home Test Kitchen

⑳ Snap Peas 'n' Ham Alfredo

prep/total time: 20 min.

1 package (24 ounces) frozen pasta, broccoli and Alfredo sauce
2 cups fresh sugar snap peas
1/4 cup water
2 cups cubed fully cooked ham
1/2 teaspoon dried oregano
1/8 teaspoon pepper

Prepare pasta and sauce according to package directions. Meanwhile, place peas and water in a microwave-safe dish. Cover and microwave on high for 2-3 minutes or until crisp-tender; drain.

Stir the peas, ham, oregano and pepper into pasta mixture; cook and stir for 3-4 minutes or until heated through. **Yield:** 4 servings.

Editor's Note: This recipe was tested in a 1,100-watt microwave.

Toss Together a Salad (tip)

You should have lettuce left over from Tuesday in the fridge. Toss together a green salad drizzled with your favorite dressing to round out this meal.

breakfast

⏱30 Fajita Frittata

prep/total time: 25 min.

1/2 pound boneless skinless chicken
    breast, cut into strips
  1 small onion, cut into thin strips
1/2 medium green pepper, cut into
    thin strips
  1 teaspoon lime juice
1/2 teaspoon salt
1/2 teaspoon ground cumin
1/2 teaspoon chili powder
  2 tablespoons canola oil
  8 eggs, beaten
  1 cup (4 ounces) shredded
    Colby-Monterey Jack cheese
Salsa and sour cream, optional

In a large ovenproof skillet, saute the chicken, onion, green pepper, lime juice, salt, cumin and chili powder in oil until chicken juices run clear.

Pour eggs over chicken mixture. Cover and cook over medium-low heat for 8-10 minutes or until eggs are nearly set. Uncover; broil 6 in. from the heat for 2-3 minutes or until eggs are set. Sprinkle with cheese. Cover and let stand for 1 minute or until cheese is melted. Serve with salsa and sour cream if desired. **Yield:** 8 servings.

This is a super-flavorful and quick entree. Though you could serve it for breakfast, whenever I ask my family what they want for dinner, this is their most popular request.
—Mary Ann Gomez
Lombard, Illinois

Raspberry-Cinnamon French Toast

prep: 10 min. + chilling **bake:** 35 min.

12 slices cinnamon bread, cubed
5 eggs, beaten
1-3/4 cups milk
1 cup packed brown sugar, *divided*
1/4 teaspoon ground cinnamon
1/4 teaspoon ground nutmeg
1/2 cup slivered almonds
1/4 cup butter, melted
2 cups fresh raspberries

Place bread cubes in a greased 13-in. x 9-in. x 2-in. baking dish. In a bowl, combine the eggs, milk, 3/4 cup brown sugar, cinnamon and nutmeg; pour over bread. Cover and refrigerate for 8 hours or overnight.

Remove from the refrigerator 30 minutes before baking. Sprinkle almonds over egg mixture. Combine butter and remaining brown sugar; drizzle over the top. Bake, uncovered, at 400° for 25 minutes. Sprinkle with raspberries. Bake 10 minutes longer or until a knife inserted near the center comes out clean. **Yield:** 6-8 servings.

This moist French toast bake is a snap to assemble the night before and bake in the morning. While it's pleasantly sweet as is, let guests drizzle raspberry syrup over the top for a finishing touch.
—Taste of Home Test Kitchen

(tip) Storing Raspberries: Refrigerate a single layer of fresh raspberries on a paper towel-lined baking sheet covered with a paper towel for up to 3 days.

Cinnamon Almond Braid

prep: 20 min. **bake:** 10 min. + cooling

1 tube (8 ounces) refrigerated
  crescent rolls
2 tablespoons plus 1/4 cup sugar,
  divided
1 teaspoon ground cinnamon
1/2 cup finely chopped slivered
  almonds
1 tablespoon butter, melted
1/4 teaspoon almond extract
ICING:
1/2 cup confectioners' sugar
1/4 teaspoon almond extract
1-1/2 to 2 teaspoons milk
1/4 teaspoon ground cinnamon

Line a 15-in. x 10-in. x 1-in. baking pan with parchment paper. Unroll crescent dough into prepared pan; seal seams and perforations. Combine 2 tablespoons sugar and cinnamon; sprinkle over dough.

Combine the almonds, butter, extract and remaining sugar; spread lengthwise down the center of dough. On each long side, cut 1-in.-wide strips about 2-1/2 in. into center. Starting at one end, fold alternating strips at an angle across filling. Pinch ends to seal. Bake at 375° for 10-15 minutes or until golden brown. Cool for 10 minutes; remove to a wire rack.

For icing, in a bowl, combine confectioners' sugar, extract and enough milk to achieve desired consistency. Drizzle over braid; sprinkle with cinnamon. Serve warm. **Yield:** 1 loaf (10 slices).

Refrigerated dough makes this pretty braid both flaky and fuss-free, while cinnamon and almonds make it simply delicious!
—Nancy Gunn
Orem, Utah

Cran-Apple Cups 30

prep/total time: 25 min.

1 tube (12.4 ounces) refrigerated
  cinnamon roll dough
1 cup apple pie filling
1/3 cup dried cranberries
1/4 teaspoon ground cinnamon

Set aside icing packet from cinnamon rolls. Place rolls in ungreased muffin cups. Bake at 400° for 8 minutes.

Meanwhile, in a small bowl, combine the pie filling, cranberries and cinnamon. With the back of a teaspoon, make an indentation in the center of each roll; fill with fruit mixture. Bake 4-5 minutes longer or until golden brown. Cool on a wire rack for 5 minutes. Drizzle with icing and serve warm. **Yield:** 8 servings.

These quick, scrumptious rolls are perfect for a holiday breakfast or brunch. And with only four ingredients, they couldn't be easier to whip up at the last minute!
—Barbara Brittain Santee, California

(tip) **Pick Other Fruit:** Try dried cherries or golden raisins in place of the cranberries for a taste twist.

(20) Cream Cheese Scrambled Eggs

prep/total time: 15 min.

1 package (3 ounces) cream cheese, softened
2 tablespoons half-and-half cream
8 eggs
1/3 cup grated Parmesan cheese
1/2 teaspoon lemon-pepper seasoning
1/8 teaspoon salt
1/2 cup real bacon bits
2 tablespoons butter

In a small mixing bowl, beat cream cheese and cream until smooth. Add the eggs, Parmesan cheese, lemon-pepper and salt; mix well. Stir in bacon. In a large skillet, melt butter; add egg mixture. Cook and stir over medium heat until eggs are completely set. **Yield:** 4 servings.

My mother-in-law introduced me to this recipe. Now it's my kids' breakfast of choice. They always ask for the "eggs with the bacon in it."
—Jacque Hunt
Heyburn, Idaho

Bacon Bits Replacement: (tip) Microwave and crumble your own bacon; use 6 to 8 slices for 1/2 cup.

Coconut Almond Muffins

prep/total time: 30 min.

- 1 cup all-purpose flour
- 1/2 cup sugar
- 1-1/4 teaspoons baking powder
- 1/4 teaspoon salt
- 1 egg
- 1/2 cup sour cream
- 1/4 cup butter, melted
- 1/4 teaspoon almond extract
- 1/2 cup flaked coconut
- 1/4 cup miniature semisweet chocolate chips
- 1/4 cup sliced almonds

Additional sugar

In a bowl, combine the flour, sugar, baking powder and salt. In another bowl, whisk the egg, sour cream, butter and extract. Stir into dry ingredients just until moistened. Fold in coconut and chocolate chips.

Fill greased muffin cups two-thirds full. Sprinkle with almonds and additional sugar. Bake at 375° for 18-20 minutes or until a toothpick comes out clean. Cool for 5 minutes before removing from pan to a wire rack. **Yield:** 6 muffins.

You might think almonds, coconut and chocolate chips are the start of a good cookie recipe, and you'd be right. But in this case, the ingredients lend delightful flavor to muffins, which have become a great favorite with my family.
—Sara Tatham, Plymouth, New Hampshire

Warm Chocolate Eggnog

prep/total time: 20 min.

- 1 quart eggnog
- 1/2 cup chocolate syrup
- 1/8 to 1/4 teaspoon ground nutmeg
- 3 teaspoons vanilla extract

Whipped cream and additional ground nutmeg

In a large saucepan, combine the eggnog, chocolate syrup and nutmeg; heat through over low heat, about 15 minutes (do not boil). Remove from the heat; stir in vanilla. Pour into mugs. Top each with a dollop of whipped cream and sprinkle of nutmeg. **Yield:** 4 servings.

Editor's Note: This recipe was tested with commercially prepared eggnog.

For a fun twist on a traditional treat, try this recipe. It's rich, sweet and simple to stir up with store-bought eggnog. *—Diane Hixon, Niceville, Florida*

30 Bacon Blueberry Scones

prep/total time: 30 min.

- 2 cups all-purpose flour
- 2 tablespoons sugar
- 2 teaspoons baking powder
- 1/2 teaspoon baking soda
- 1/2 teaspoon salt
- 1/2 teaspoon ground cinnamon
- 1/3 cup cold butter
- 3/4 cup buttermilk
- 1 tablespoon vegetable oil
- 1 cup fresh *or* frozen blueberries
- 4 bacon strips, cooked and crumbled
- 1 egg
- 1 tablespoon milk

In a large bowl, combine the first six ingredients. Cut in butter until mixture resembles coarse crumbs. In a small bowl, whisk buttermilk and oil; add to crumb mixture. Stir in blueberries and bacon.

Turn onto a floured surface; knead 10 times. Pat into an 8-in. circle. Cut into eight wedges. Separate wedges and place on a greased baking sheet.

In a small bowl, beat egg and milk; brush over scones. Bake at 425° for 12-15 minutes or until golden brown. Serve warm. **Yield:** 8 servings.

Editor's Note: If using frozen blueberries, do not thaw before adding to batter.

Blueberry scones are a nice alternative to muffins in the morning. And the bacon in these scones adds a savory twist, making them a nice addition to any brunch.
—Patricia Harmon
Baden, Pennsylvania

- - - - - - - - - - - - - - -

Sprinkle Them With Sugar: (tip) After brushing the top of these scones with the egg mixture, sprinkle with sugar for a sweeter taste and a little sparkle.

Strawberry Banana Omelet ⑳

prep/total time: 20 min.

3 tablespoons butter, *divided*
2 tablespoons brown sugar
1/8 teaspoon ground cinnamon
2 medium firm bananas, sliced
1/4 teaspoon vanilla extract
1-1/2 cups sliced fresh strawberries
6 eggs
2 tablespoons water
1/2 teaspoon salt
Confectioners' sugar

In a small saucepan, heat 1 tablespoon butter, brown sugar and cinnamon over medium heat until sugar is dissolved. Add bananas and vanilla; toss to coat. Remove from the heat; stir in strawberries. Set aside.

In a large bowl, beat the eggs, water and salt. Heat remaining butter in a 10-in. nonstick skillet over medium heat; add egg mixture. As eggs set, lift edges, letting uncooked portion flow underneath.

When eggs are almost set, spread two-thirds of fruit mixture over one side; fold omelet over filling. Cover and cook for 1-2 minutes or until heated through. Slide onto a serving plate; top with remaining fruit mixture and dust with confectioners' sugar. **Yield:** 2-3 servings.

You may be surprised by the sweet, fruity filling we whipped up for this unusual version of the classic morning mainstay.
—Taste of Home
Test Kitchen

Creamy Ham 'n' Egg Casserole

prep: 15 min. **bake:** 20 min.

2 medium cooked potatoes, peeled and sliced
4 hard-cooked eggs, chopped
1 cup diced fully cooked ham
1/2 teaspoon salt
1/4 teaspoon pepper
1 egg
1-1/2 cups (12 ounces) sour cream
1/4 cup dry bread crumbs
1 tablespoon butter, melted

In a large bowl, combine the potatoes, eggs, ham, salt and pepper. Combine the egg and sour cream; add to potato mixture and gently toss to coat. Transfer to a greased 11-in. x 7-in. x 2-in. baking dish.

Toss bread crumbs and butter; sprinkle over casserole. Bake, uncovered, at 350° for 20 minutes or until mixture reaches 160°. **Yield:** 6 servings.

Have leftover cooked potatoes or eggs on hand? Here's a terrific way to use them up! This breakfast main dish is a great way to fill up family members before they leave for work, school or wherever they need to be.
—Dixie Terry
Goreville, Illinois

- - - - - - - - - - - - - - -

Keeping Cooked Eggs: Hard-cooked eggs should be refrigerated no more than a week. **(tip)**

Apple Puff Pancake 30

prep/total time: 25 min.

1/3 cup butter
1 cup all-purpose flour
4 eggs
1 cup milk
Dash salt
1 can (21 ounces) apple *or* peach
    pie filling
Toasted walnuts, optional

Place butter in a 10-in. ovenproof skillet. Place in a 425° oven until melted. In a large mixing bowl, beat the flour, eggs, milk and salt until smooth. Leaving 1 tablespoon melted butter in the skillet, pour the remaining butter into the batter; mix until blended. Pour batter into hot skillet. Bake for 15-20 minutes or until edges are golden brown.

In a small saucepan, warm pie filling over low heat until heated through. Pour into center of puff pancake. Sprinkle with walnuts if desired. Serve immediately. **Yield:** 4 servings.

This thick and puffy pancake has such a pretty presentation that it gets high praise from family and company alike. For an extra-special touch, try topping each serving with warm pancake syrup and a dollop of whipped cream.
—*Linda Hubbuch*
Versailles, Kentucky

(30) Fiesta Scrambled Eggs

prep/total time: 30 min.

1/2   **cup chopped onion**
1/4   **cup chopped sweet red pepper**
1   **jalapeno pepper, seeded and chopped**
8   **bacon strips, cooked and crumbled**
8   **eggs, lightly beaten**
1   **cup (4 ounces) shredded cheddar cheese,** *divided*
1/2   **teaspoon salt**
1/8   **teaspoon pepper**
Salsa

In a large nonstick skillet coated with non-stick cooking spray, saute the onion and peppers until tender. Sprinkle with bacon. Pour eggs over the top; sprinkle with 1/2 cup cheese, salt and pepper. Cook over medium heat, stirring occasionally, until eggs are completely set. Sprinkle with remaining cheese. Serve with salsa. **Yield:** 6 servings.

Editor's Note: When cutting or seeding hot peppers, use rubber or plastic gloves to protect your hands. Avoid touching your face.

I love to fix this spicy scrambled egg dish for friends and family. It's a meal in itself, but I serve it with muffins or biscuits, fresh fruit, juice and coffee.
—*Kay Kropff*
Canyon, Texas

Honey Fruit Salad ⑩

prep/total time: 10 min.

2 medium firm bananas, chopped
2 cups fresh blueberries
2 cups fresh raspberries
2 cups sliced fresh strawberries
5 tablespoons honey
1 teaspoon lemon juice
3/4 teaspoon poppy seeds

In a large bowl, combine the bananas and berries. In a small bowl, combine the honey, lemon juice and poppy seeds. Pour over fruit and toss to coat. **Yield:** 8 servings.

Though fresh fruit steals the show in this morning medley, the subtle honey sauce makes it an especially sweet treat. It takes just 10 minutes to assemble this easy salad, which tastes so good with brunch.
—*Dorothy Dinnean Harrison, Arkansas*

(tip) **Fruit Options:** Don't have these fruits on hand? Try blackberries, mangoes or peaches instead.

Speedy Sausage Squares

prep: 15 min. **bake:** 30 min.

- 1 tube (8 ounces) refrigerated crescent rolls
- 1 pound bulk pork sausage
- 1/4 cup chopped onion
- 6 eggs, lightly beaten
- 3/4 cup milk
- 2 tablespoons chopped green pepper
- 1/2 teaspoon dried oregano
- 1/2 teaspoon pepper
- 1/4 teaspoon garlic salt
- 1 cup (4 ounces) shredded part-skim mozzarella cheese

Unroll crescent dough into a greased 13-in. x 9-in. x 2-in. baking dish; seal seams and perforations. Bake at 375° for 6 minutes or until golden brown.

Meanwhile, in a skillet, cook sausage and onion over medium heat until meat is no longer pink; drain. In a bowl, combine the eggs, milk, green pepper, oregano, pepper and garlic salt; pour over crust. Sprinkle with sausage mixture. Bake for 15-20 minutes. Sprinkle with cheese; bake 5 minutes longer or until cheese is melted. **Yield:** 12 servings.

Whenever I want to serve something special for a family brunch, this is usually what I prepare. I'll get the ingredients together the night before, so it's a snap to bake the next morning.
—Miriam Yoder
Houstonia, Missouri

- - - - - - - - - - - - - - - -

Keep It Lean: Drain, rinse and pat cooked pork sausage dry with paper towels before using in a recipe to cut calories and fat.

Almond Chip Scones 30

prep/total time: 30 min.

3-1/2 cups all-purpose flour
2 tablespoons sugar
5 teaspoons baking powder
1 teaspoon salt
1/2 cup cold butter
4 eggs
1 cup heavy whipping cream
1-1/2 to 2 teaspoons almond extract
1 cup (6 ounces) semisweet chocolate chips
1/2 cup slivered almonds, toasted

In a large bowl, combine the flour, sugar, baking powder and salt. Cut in butter until the mixture resembles coarse crumbs. In a bowl, whisk 3 eggs, cream and extract; add to crumb mixture just until moistened. Gently stir in chips and almonds. Turn onto a floured surface; knead 6-8 times.

On a greased baking sheet, pat the dough into a 10-1/2-in. circle, about 3/4 in. thick. Cut into eight wedges. Beat remaining egg; brush over dough. Slightly separate wedges. Bake at 425° for 10-15 minutes or until golden brown. Serve warm. **Yield:** 8 servings.

I often triple the recipe for these moist scones. You can try blueberries instead of the chocolate chips and almonds. Or cut the dough into strips like biscotti, bake them and dip them into coffee.
—Heidi Rowley
Baton Rouge, Louisiana

Chocolate Chip Pancakes

prep: 15 min. **cook:** 5 min. per batch

2 cups biscuit/baking mix
2 tablespoons instant chocolate drink mix
2 teaspoons baking powder
1 egg
1 cup milk
1/2 cup sour cream
1/4 cup miniature semisweet chocolate chips
Maple syrup and butter, optional

In a large bowl, combine the biscuit mix, drink mix and baking powder. Combine the egg, milk and sour cream; stir into dry ingredients just until moistened. Fold in chocolate chips.

Pour batter by 1/4 cupfuls onto a greased hot griddle. Turn when bubbles form on top; cook until second side is golden brown. Serve with maple syrup and butter if desired. **Yield:** 11 pancakes.

Mornings will get off to a great start with these yummy double-chocolate pancakes. The whole family will rave about this quick-and-easy breakfast.
—Taste of Home Test Kitchen

Simple Swap:
You can use chocolate milk in place of the drink mix and milk in this recipe.

(tip)

Spicy Maple Sausages
prep/total time: 15 min.

   2 packages (7 ounces *each*)
      brown-and-serve sausage links
 1/4 cup maple syrup
 1/4 cup honey
   2 teaspoons Dijon mustard
 1/2 teaspoon ground cinnamon
 1/2 teaspoon cayenne pepper

In a large skillet, cook sausage links until browned; drain. Combine the remaining ingredients; stir into skillet. Bring to a boil; cook and stir for 2-3 minutes or until sausages are glazed. **Yield:** 6-8 servings.

Wake up your family's taste buds with this easy treatment for breakfast sausages. Just five ingredients are needed for the glaze. —Taste of Home Test Kitchen

Jazzed-Up French Toast Sticks
prep/total time: 25 min.

   4 ounces spreadable strawberry cream
      cheese
 12 French toast sticks
   1 snack-size cup (4 ounces) mixed fruit
   1 tablespoon orange juice
Sliced fresh strawberries, optional

Spread cream cheese over six French toast sticks, about 1 tablespoon on each; top with remaining sticks. Place in a greased 9-in. square baking pan. Bake at 400° for 15-17 minutes or until golden brown.

    Meanwhile, in a blender, combine mixed fruit and orange juice; cover and process until smooth. Serve with French toast sticks. Garnish with strawberries if desired. **Yield:** 3 servings.

Store-bought French toast sticks are spread with strawberry cream cheese to make this fun, fast breakfast fare.   **—Anna Free, Bradner, Ohio**

Toffee-Flavored Coffee
prep/total time: 15 min.

 1/2 cup heavy whipping cream
   1 tablespoon confectioners' sugar
 1/2 cup milk chocolate toffee bits
   5 cups hot brewed coffee
   2 tablespoons butterscotch ice cream
      topping

In a small mixing bowl, beat cream until it begins to thicken. Add confectioners' sugar; beat until stiff peaks form. Stir toffee bits into coffee; let stand for 30 seconds. Strain and discard any undissolved toffee bits. Pour coffee into mugs; top with whipped cream and drizzle with butterscotch topping. **Yield:** 5 servings.

With its special toffee flavor, this java drink makes mornings pleasantly perk along. Or treat yourself to a cup in the afternoon as a quick pick-me-up.
     —Taste of Home Test Kitchen

(20) Bacon 'n' Egg Bagels

prep/total time: 20 min.

4 bagels, split and toasted
1/2 cup garden vegetable cheese spread
1/2 cup sliced pimiento-stuffed olives
8 bacon strips, halved
4 eggs
4 slices Muenster cheese

Spread each bagel half with cheese spread. Place olives on bagel bottoms; set aside.

In a large skillet, cook bacon over medium heat until crisp. Using a slotted spoon, remove to paper towels; drain, reserving 3 table-spoons drippings. Heat drippings over medium-hot heat. Add eggs; reduce heat to low. Fry until whites are completely set and yolks begin to thicken but are not hard. Place an egg on each bagel bottom. Layer with cheese, bacon and bagel tops. **Yield:** 4 servings.

Wake up taste buds with these breakfast sandwiches. Better than fast-food fare, the savory bagels with vegetable cream cheese and zesty olives will get them to the table in a hurry.
—Chris and Jenny Thackray
Corpus Christi, Texas

Change Up The Cheese: (tip)
For a change of pace, prepare the bagels with another flavor of cream cheese.

Fruit Smoothies 🕙
prep/total time: 5 min.

3/4 cup milk
1/2 cup orange juice
1/2 cup unsweetened applesauce
  1 small ripe banana, halved
1/2 cup frozen unsweetened
      raspberries
  7 to 10 ice cubes

In a blender, combine all ingredients; cover and process until smooth. Pour into chilled glasses; serve immediately. **Yield:** 3 servings.

I came up with this recipe when hanging around in the kitchen one day. These smoothies are so delicious, they taste like they came from a smoothie shop.
—Bryce Sickich
New Port Richey, Florida

(30) Chocolate Croissants

prep/total time: 25 min.

12 unsliced croissants
2 cups milk chocolate chips
1/3 cup sugar
1 teaspoon cornstarch
1 teaspoon ground cinnamon
1 cup milk
4 eggs, lightly beaten
1/2 cup half-and-half cream
3 teaspoons vanilla extract

Cut a slit into the side of each croissant; fill each with about 2 tablespoons chocolate chips. In a shallow bowl, combine the sugar, cornstarch and cinnamon; whisk in milk until smooth. Whisk in eggs, cream and vanilla.

Dip croissants into egg mixture. Place in two greased 15-in. x 10-in. x 1-in. baking pans. Bake at 400° for 7-9 minutes or until golden brown. Serve warm. **Yield:** 1 dozen.

From time to time, we have stuffed French toast made from rich buttery brioche. One Father's Day when I wanted to make it for my husband, the store was out of brioche, so I tried croissants instead. They turned out to be even simpler to use.
—Phyllis Johnston
Fayetteville, Tennessee

Tomato Asparagus Frittata 30

prep/total time: 25 min.

1/4 pound fresh asparagus, trimmed
and cut in half
6 eggs
8 bacon strips, cooked and
crumbled
1 cup sliced fresh mushrooms
1/3 cup chopped onion
1/4 cup butter
1 medium tomato, sliced
1 cup (4 ounces) shredded cheddar
cheese

Place asparagus in a steamer basket; place in
a saucepan over 1 in. of water. Bring to a
boil; cover and steam for 4-5 minutes or until
crisp-tender. Drain and set aside.

In a bowl, whisk eggs until frothy; stir in
bacon. In a large skillet, saute mushrooms
and onion in butter until tender. Add egg
mixture. As eggs begin to set, lift edges, letting uncooked portion flow underneath until
eggs are soft-set.

Arrange asparagus over egg mixture to
resemble spokes of a wheel. Top with tomato
slices. Cover and cook over medium-low heat
until eggs are set. Sprinkle with cheese.
Remove from the heat. Cover and let stand for
3-4 minutes or until cheese is slightly melted. **Yield:** 6-8 servings.

*With sliced tomatoes and
fresh asparagus spears on
top, this hearty garden
frittata comes together
in no time at all.*
*—Barbara Nowakowski
North Tonawanda,
New York*

(tip) **Faster
Frittata:** To
streamline the
prep, substitute real bacon
bits and use sliced
mushrooms and diced onions
from the produce section
of your grocery store.

⑩ Homemade Maple Syrup

prep/total time: 10 min.

- 1 cup sugar
- 1 cup packed brown sugar
- 1 cup water
- 1 teaspoon maple flavoring

In a small saucepan, combine the sugars and water. Bring to a boil; cook and stir for 2 minutes. Remove from the heat; stir in maple flavoring. Refrigerate leftovers. **Yield:** 2 cups.

My husband has fond memories of this recipe. Every Sunday morning, his dad would get up early to make the family pancakes and syrup. They didn't have much money, but the kids never knew that. What they do remember is that their dad always had time to make their Sundays extra special. —Lorrie McCurdy
Farmington, New Mexico

⑳ Light 'n' Crispy Waffles

prep/total time: 20 min.

- 2 cups biscuit/baking mix
- 2 eggs, lightly beaten
- 1/2 cup vegetable oil
- 1 cup club soda

In a small bowl, combine the biscuit mix, eggs and oil. Add club soda and stir until smooth. Bake in a preheated waffle iron according to manufacturer's directions until golden brown. **Yield:** 12 waffles.

Club soda gives these crisp golden waffles a wonderful fluffy texture. —Taste of Home
Test Kitchen

Creamy Hazelnut Dip 20

prep/total time: 15 min.

2 packages (3 ounces *each*) cream cheese, softened
1/2 cup chocolate hazelnut spread
1 teaspoon vanilla extract
1/2 cup confectioners' sugar
1 cup heavy whipping cream, whipped
1/2 cup chopped hazelnuts
Fresh strawberries, biscotti and Milano cookies

In a small mixing bowl, combine the cream cheese, chocolate hazelnut spread and vanilla. Beat in confectioners' sugar until smooth. Fold in whipped cream and hazelnuts. Serve with strawberries, biscotti and cookies. **Yield:** about 3 cups.

This rich chocolate dip is a sweet way to begin your morning. With crunchy hazelnuts stirred into the mousse-like mixture, it's wonderful with fresh fruit or cookies.
—Taste of Home Test Kitchen

(tip) **Sweet Spread:** Not quite sure where to get the chocolate hazelnut spread for the fruit dip? Jars of Nutella, a popular brand, can be found near the peanut butter and jelly at most larger grocery stores.

Fruit Slush

prep: 20 min. + freezing

3 cups water
1 cup sugar
1 can (20 ounces) crushed pineapple, undrained
1 can (6 ounces) frozen orange juice concentrate, thawed
1 medium ripe peach, chopped *or* 2/3 cup sliced frozen peaches, thawed and chopped

In a large saucepan over medium heat, bring water and sugar to a boil. Remove from the heat. Cool for 10 minutes.

Add the pineapple, orange juice concentrate and peach; stir well. Pour into a freezer container; freeze for at least 12 hours or overnight. May be frozen for up to 3 months. Remove from freezer 1 hour before serving. **Yield:** 6-8 servings.

I'm a busy mom and do all that I can before expecting company. This sweet citrus slush is easy to make ahead and tastes so refreshing.
—Martha Miller
Fredericksburg, Ohio

Breakfast Wraps 20

prep/total time: 15 min.

6 eggs
2 tablespoons milk
1/4 teaspoon pepper
1 tablespoon vegetable oil
1 cup (4 ounces) shredded cheddar cheese
3/4 cup diced fully cooked ham
4 flour tortillas (8 inches), warmed

In a small bowl, whisk the eggs, milk and pepper. In a large skillet, heat oil. Add the egg mixture; cook and stir over medium heat until the eggs are completely set. Stir in the cheese and ham.

Spoon egg mixture down the center of each tortilla; roll up. Serve immediately, or wrap in plastic wrap and freeze in a resealable plastic bag.

To use frozen wraps: Thaw in the refrigerator overnight. Remove plastic wrap; wrap tortilla in a moist microwave-safe paper towel. Microwave on high for 30-60 seconds or until heated through. Serve immediately. **Yield:** 4 servings.

We like quick and simple morning meals during the week, and these wraps are great when they're prepared ahead of time. With just a minute in the microwave, a hot breakfast is ready to eat!
—Betty Kleberger
Florissant, Missouri

(tip) **Storing Eggs:** Store eggs in their carton on an inside refrigerator shelf, not in a compartment on the door. The carton cushions the eggs and helps prevent moisture loss and odor absorption.

Caramel Sweet Rolls

prep: 10 min. **bake:** 25 min.

1/2 **cup packed brown sugar**
1/3 **cup heavy whipping cream**
1/4 **cup chopped walnuts**
1 **tube (11 ounces) refrigerated breadsticks**
2 **tablespoons sugar**
1 **teaspoon ground cinnamon**

In a small bowl, combine brown sugar and cream until sugar is dissolved. Spread into a greased 8-in. square baking dish. Sprinkle with walnuts.

On a lightly floured surface, unroll breadstick dough (do not separate). Combine sugar and cinnamon; sprinkle over dough. Reroll, starting with a short end. Cut along breadstick scored lines. Place cut side down in prepared pan.

Bake at 350° for 25-30 minutes or until golden brown. Cool for 1 minute before inverting onto a serving plate. Serve warm. **Yield:** 6 servings.

Our family loves sweet rolls. This is my favorite recipe because it calls for a tube of ready-made breadstick dough, so it's so easy. The sweet rolls take just minutes to assemble but taste like you spent hours making them.
—Krista Smith
Mentone, California

- - - - - - - - - - - - - - -

Warming Up Rolls: To reheat these sweet rolls, wrap in foil coated with nonstick cooking spray. Reheat in a 350° oven for a few minutes or until warm. **tip**

Fruity Baked Oatmeal

prep: 15 min. **bake:** 35 min.

3 cups quick-cooking oats
1 cup packed brown sugar
2 teaspoons baking powder
1 teaspoon salt
1/2 teaspoon ground cinnamon
2 eggs, lightly beaten
1 cup milk
1/2 cup butter, melted
3/4 cup chopped peeled tart apple
1/3 cup chopped fresh *or* frozen peaches
1/3 cup fresh *or* frozen blueberries
Additional milk, optional

In a large bowl, combine the oats, brown sugar, baking powder, salt and cinnamon. Combine the eggs, milk and butter; add to the dry ingredients. Stir in the apple, peaches and blueberries.

Pour into an 8-in. square baking dish coated with nonstick cooking spray. Bake, uncovered, at 350° for 35-40 minutes or until a knife inserted near the center comes out clean. Cut into squares. Serve with milk if desired. **Yield:** 9 servings.

Editor's Note: If using frozen blueberries, do not thaw before adding to batter.

This is my husband's favorite breakfast treat and the ultimate comfort food. It's warm, filling and always a hit when I serve it to guests.
—Karen Schroeder
Kankakee, Illinois

⑩ Cherry Berry Smoothies

prep/total time: 5 min.

1-1/2 cups unsweetened apple juice
1 cup frozen unsweetened raspberries
1 cup frozen pitted dark sweet cherries
1-1/2 cups raspberry sherbet

In a blender, combine apple juice, raspberries and cherries. Add sherbet; cover and process until well blended. Pour into chilled glasses; serve immediately. **Yield:** 4 servings.

You need just four ingredients to blend together these super-fast smoothies for breakfast. Try whipping them up on a hot summer day for a cool and refreshing treat.
—Macy Plummer
Avon, Indiana

Fruity Peanut Butter Pitas

prep/total time: 5 min.

- 1/4 cup peanut butter
- 1/8 teaspoon *each* ground allspice, cinnamon and nutmeg
- 1 whole wheat pita bread, cut in half
- 1/2 medium apple, thinly sliced
- 1/2 medium firm banana, sliced

In a bowl, blend peanut butter, allspice, cinnamon and nutmeg. Spread inside pita bread halves; fill with apple and banana slices. **Yield:** 2 servings.

My kids often request these tasty sandwiches. They haven't noticed these pitas are good for them, too.
—Kim Holmes, Emerald Park, Saskatchewan

Citrus Spiced Coffee

prep/total time: 15 min.

- 3/4 cup ground coffee
- 1 teaspoon grated lemon peel
- 1 cup water
- 3/4 cup packed brown sugar
- 3 cinnamon sticks (3 inches)
- 2 fresh orange slices
- 2 tablespoons unsweetened pineapple juice
- 1/2 teaspoon vanilla extract

Place the coffee grounds in a filter or basket of a coffeemaker; add lemon peel. Prepare 9 cups brewed coffee according to manufacturer's directions.

In a small saucepan, combine water, brown sugar, cinnamon sticks, orange slices, pineapple juice and vanilla. Cook and stir over medium heat until sugar is dissolved. Strain; discard cinnamon and oranges. Pour sugar mixture into mugs; add coffee. Stir. **Yield:** 9 servings.

Brewed with lemon peel, then stirred into mugs with a pineapple-sugar mixture, this coffee adds zest to sunrise schedules. —Taste of Home Test Kitchen

Breakfast Parfaits

prep/total time: 10 min.

- 2 cups pineapple chunks
- 1 cup fresh *or* frozen raspberries
- 1 cup (8 ounces) vanilla yogurt
- 1 cup sliced ripe banana
- 1/2 cup chopped dates *or* raisins
- 1/4 cup sliced almonds

In four parfait glasses or serving dishes, layer the pineapple, raspberries, yogurt, banana and dates. Sprinkle with almonds. Serve immediately. **Yield:** 4 servings.

These colorful treats are layered with yogurt, chewy dates and other fruit, and crunchy nuts. This is one morning meal the whole family will enjoy.
—Adell Meyer, Madison, Wisconsin

Pear-Pecan Sausage Quiche

prep: 15 min. **bake:** 35 min.

1/2 pound bulk hot Italian sausage
1/3 cup chopped sweet onion
  1 medium pear, sliced
  1 unbaked pastry shell (9 inches)
1/3 cup chopped pecans
  4 eggs
1-1/2 cups half-and-half cream
1/2 teaspoon salt
1/2 teaspoon dried thyme
1/8 teaspoon ground nutmeg
  1 cup (4 ounces) shredded cheddar
    cheese
  8 pecan halves

In a large skillet, cook sausage and onion over medium heat for 4-5 minutes or until meat is no longer pink; drain. Arrange pear slices in pastry shell; top with the sausage mixture. Sprinkle with chopped pecans. In a large bowl, whisk the eggs, cream, salt, thyme and nutmeg. Stir in cheese. Pour over sausage mixture.

Bake at 350° for 35-40 minutes or until a knife inserted near the center comes out clean and crust is golden brown. Garnish with pecan halves. Let stand for 5 minutes before slicing. **Yield:** 8 servings.

This quiche is a delightful addition to brunch. It's savory from the spicy sausage yet sweet from the sliced pear.
—Patricia Harmon
Baden, Pennsylvania

Doneness Test: Test egg dishes containing beaten eggs—like quiche, strata or custard—for doneness by inserting a knife near the center of the dish. If the knife comes out clean, the eggs are cooked.

tip

French Toast Supreme ⏱20

prep/total time: 15 min.

8   slices Texas toast
4   slices Canadian bacon
4   slices Monterey Jack cheese
1   egg
1/2 cup refrigerated French vanilla
    nondairy creamer
Confectioners' sugar, optional
1/4 cup seedless raspberry jam

On four slices of Texas toast, place one slice of bacon and one slice of cheese; top with remaining Texas toast. In a shallow bowl, whisk egg and creamer. Dip sandwiches into egg mixture.

On a hot griddle or large skillet coated with nonstick cooking spray, cook sandwiches for 2-3 minutes on each side or until golden brown. Sprinkle with confectioners' sugar if desired. Serve with jam. **Yield:** 4 servings.

I often use thick slices of French bread or homemade white bread when fixing these sandwiches. I served them with a fresh fruit salad at brunch, and everyone asked me for the recipe. It's easy to double or triple for a hungry crowd.
—Elaine Bonica
Bethel, Maine

⏱20 Pecan-Stuffed Waffles

prep/total time: 15 min.

8 frozen waffles
2 packages (3 ounces *each*) cream
  cheese, softened
1/2 cup packed brown sugar
1-1/2 teaspoons ground cinnamon
1 teaspoon vanilla extract
1/2 cup chopped pecans
1 cup maple syrup
Confectioners' sugar
4 fresh strawberries, cut in half

Toast waffles according to package directions. In a small mixing bowl, beat the cream cheese, brown sugar, cinnamon and vanilla until smooth. Stir in pecans. Spread over four waffles; top with remaining waffles. Drizzle with syrup. Sprinkle with confectioners' sugar; garnish each with a strawberry. **Yield:** 4 servings.

This is a great recipe for entertaining because it's easy yet extremely impressive. The creamy brown sugar and pecan filling between the waffles is delectable!
—Jenny Flake
Gilbert, Arizona

Sweet Treat: ⓣⓘⓟ
These waffles
would not only
be popular for breakfast,
but dessert as well!

Spicy Scrambled Egg Sandwiches ③⓪

prep/total time: 30 min.

1/3 cup chopped green pepper
1/4 cup chopped onion
3 eggs
4 egg whites
1 tablespoon water
1/4 teaspoon salt
1/4 teaspoon ground mustard
1/8 teaspoon pepper
1/8 teaspoon hot pepper sauce
1/3 cup fresh *or* frozen corn, thawed
1/4 cup real bacon bits
4 English muffins, split and toasted

In a 10-in. skillet coated with nonstick cooking spray, cook green pepper and onion over medium heat until tender, about 8 minutes.

In a large bowl, whisk the eggs, egg whites, water, salt, mustard, pepper and hot pepper sauce. Pour into skillet. Add corn and bacon; cook and stir until the eggs are completely set. Spoon onto English muffin bottoms; replace tops. Serve immediately. **Yield:** 4 servings.

These breakfast sandwiches are packed with veggies, good taste and easy-to-swallow nutrition!
—Helen Vail
Glenside, Pennsylvania

⏱30 Morning Cinnamon Rolls

prep/total time: 25 min.

1 tube (8 ounces) refrigerated
   reduced-fat crescent rolls
Sugar substitute equivalent to 1/2 cup
   sugar, *divided*
1/2 teaspoon ground cinnamon
1/4 cup confectioners' sugar
1 tablespoon fat-free milk

Unroll crescent dough into a rectangle; seal seams and perforations. Combine half of the sugar substitute and the cinnamon; sprinkle over dough. Roll up jelly-roll style, starting with a long side; seal edge. Cut into eight slices. Place rolls cut side down in a 9-in. round baking pan coated with nonstick cooking spray. Bake at 375° for 12-15 minutes or until golden brown.

In a small bowl, combine the confectioners' sugar, milk and remaining sugar substitute; drizzle over the warm rolls. **Yield:** 8 servings.

Editor's Note: This recipe was tested with Splenda Sugar Blend for Baking.

Convenient crescent roll dough helps hurry along these yummy glazed rolls. I found this recipe in a cookbook, but slimmed it down by using sugar substitute instead of sugar.
—Helen Lipko
Martinsburg, Pennsylvania

soups & sandwiches

Veggie Bean Soup, pg. 127
Guacamole Chicken Wraps, pg. 118

⑳ Grilled Sourdough Clubs

prep/total time: 20 min.

12 slices sourdough bread
6 slices cheddar cheese
1/2 pound thinly sliced deli turkey
1/4 teaspoon garlic powder
1/2 pound thinly sliced deli ham
12 bacon strips, cooked and drained
2 tablespoons butter, softened

On six slices of bread, layer cheese and turkey; sprinkle with garlic powder. Top with ham, bacon and remaining bread. Spread butter over the top and bottom of each sandwich. Cook on an indoor grill or panini maker for 3-4 minutes or until bread is toasted and cheese is melted. **Yield:** 6 servings.

Filled with ham, turkey, bacon and cheese, these hearty sandwiches appeal to all ages and grill up in no time.
—Kristina Franklin
Clarkston, Washington

Try Another Turkey: If your deli offers garlic herb turkey breast, you can substitute that and eliminate the garlic powder.

tip

Shrimp 'n' Black Bean Chili 30

prep/total time: 25 min.

1/2 cup chopped onion
1/2 cup chopped green pepper
1 tablespoon canola oil
1 can (15 ounces) black beans, rinsed and drained
1 can (14-1/2 ounces) diced tomatoes, undrained
1 cup chicken broth
1/3 cup picante sauce
1 teaspoon ground cumin
1/2 teaspoon dried basil
1 pound cooked medium shrimp, peeled and deveined
Hot cooked rice, optional

In a large saucepan, saute onion and green pepper in oil for 4-5 minutes or until crisp-tender. Stir in the beans, tomatoes, broth, picante sauce, cumin and basil. Reduce heat; simmer, uncovered, for 10-15 minutes or until heated through. Add shrimp; simmer 3-4 minutes longer or until heated through. Serve with rice if desired. **Yield:** 6 servings.

It's not spicy, but this flavorful chili is sure to warm you up on cold winter evenings. Since this recipe calls for cooked shrimp and canned goods, it's very quick to prepare.
—Elizabeth Hunt
Kirbyville, Texas

⑳ Egg Drop Soup

prep/total time: 15 min.

3 cups chicken broth
1 tablespoon cornstarch
2 tablespoons cold water
1 egg, lightly beaten
1 green onion, sliced

In a large saucepan, bring broth to a boil over medium heat. Combine cornstarch and water until smooth; gradually stir into broth. Bring to a boil; cook and stir for 2 minutes or until thickened.

Reduce heat. Drizzle beaten egg into hot broth, stirring constantly. Remove from the heat; stir in onion. **Yield:** 4 servings.

There are many recipe variations of egg drop soup, but we like the addition of cornstarch to thicken this version and give it a rich, golden color.
—Amy Corlew-Sherlock
Lapeer, Michigan

Special Sandwich Loaves 🕒30

prep/total time: 30 min.

2 loaves (1 pound *each*) French bread
10 slices deli smoked turkey, halved
10 slices deli roast beef, halved
20 small lettuce leaves
10 slices Colby-Monterey Jack cheese, halved
10 slices cheddar cheese, halved
2 cups roasted sweet red peppers, drained, sliced and patted dry
40 mild banana peppers, drained, sliced and patted dry

GARLIC-LIME MAYONNAISE:
1 cup mayonnaise
1/2 cup sour cream
1 teaspoon lime juice

1/2 teaspoon minced garlic
1/4 teaspoon chili powder
1 bottle (5 ounces) submarine sandwich dressing

Cut each loaf into 22 slices, leaving slices attached at the bottom (cut off and discard end pieces). Between every other slice of bread, place a piece of turkey and beef, a lettuce leaf, a piece of each kind of cheese, red peppers and banana peppers.

In a small bowl, whisk the mayonnaise, sour cream, lime juice, garlic and chili powder. To serve, cut completely through the bread between the plain bread sides. Serve with mayonnaise mixture and submarine dressing. **Yield:** 20 sandwiches.

These satisfying sub sandwiches look so appetizing yet are a study in simplicity. Offering the seasoned mayonnaise and submarine sandwich dressing on the side makes it easy for guests to personalize their helpings and serve themselves.
—Taste of Home Test Kitchen

(tip) **Shopping for Salad Dressing:** Look for bottles of submarine salad dressing in the deli section of many grocery stores. Or use Italian dressing as an easy alternative.

⑩ Guacamole Chicken Wraps

prep/total time: 10 min.

1/2 cup guacamole
4 spinach tortillas (8 inches)
1/2 cup salsa
1 cup (4 ounces) shredded Mexican cheese blend
12 ounces ready-to-use Southwestern chicken strips
4 lettuce leaves

Spread guacamole over half of each tortilla. Layer with salsa, cheese, chicken and lettuce to within 2 in. of edges. Roll up tightly.
Yield: 4 servings.

Convenience items, including seasoned chicken strips, prepared guacamole and jarred salsa, add great Southwestern flavor to these roll-ups.
—Taste of Home Test Kitchen

Good Uses for Guacamole: (tip) Guacamole can be used as a dip, sauce, topping or side dish. It must be covered tightly to prevent discoloration.

Hot Turkey Sandwiches

prep/total time: 10 min.

- 1 package (6 ounces) chicken stuffing mix
- 4 slices white bread, toasted
- 1 pound thinly sliced deli turkey
- 1 cup turkey gravy

Prepare stuffing mix according to package directions. Place the toast on a large microwave-safe plate; top each with turkey, stuffing and gravy. Microwave, uncovered, on high for 30-40 seconds or until heated through. **Yield:** 4 servings.

Editor's Note: This recipe was tested in a 1,100-watt microwave.

I like to team these tasty, open-faced sandwiches with cranberry sauce and green beans for a filling meal.
—Margery Bryan, Moses Lake, Washington

Ham and Mango Wraps

prep/total time: 25 min.

- 1/3 cup sour cream
- 1/3 cup mayonnaise
- 2 tablespoons minced fresh basil
- 2 tablespoons minced chives
- 1 tablespoon lemon juice
- 1/8 teaspoon salt
- 1/8 teaspoon pepper
- 3 cups cubed fully cooked ham (about 1 pound)
- 2 to 3 medium mangoes, peeled, chopped and patted dry (about 2 cups)
- 6 flour tortillas (10 inches), warmed

In a large bowl, combine the first seven ingredients. Stir in the ham and mangoes. Spoon about 2/3 cup down the center of each tortilla; roll up tightly. **Yield:** 6 servings.

The unusual pairing of savory ham and sweet, juicy mangoes in these luscious wraps makes a cool summer lunch. —Bonnie Austin, Grenada, Mississippi

⑩ Tortilla Soup

prep/total time: 10 min.

- 1 can (10-1/2 ounces) condensed chicken with rice soup, undiluted
- 1-1/3 cups water
- 1 cup salsa
- 1 cup canned pinto beans, rinsed and drained
- 1 cup canned black beans, rinsed and drained
- 1 cup frozen corn
- 1 cup frozen diced cooked chicken
- 1 teaspoon ground cumin

Crushed tortilla chips, shredded cheddar cheese and sour cream

In a large saucepan, combine the first eight ingredients. Cook over medium-high heat for 5-7 minutes or until heated through. Serve with tortilla chips, cheese and sour cream. **Yield:** 5 servings.

Flavorful toppings jazz up this no-fuss soup that has Mexican flair. The recipe for this sure-to-please soup was given to me by a friend. I make it often for company, and everyone asks for the recipe.
—Michelle Larson, Greentown, Indiana

30 Basil Red Pepper Sandwiches

prep/total time: 25 min.

1 loaf (1 pound) unsliced Italian bread
1 to 2 teaspoons grated lemon peel
2 tablespoons plus 1 teaspoon olive oil, *divided*
8 ounces sliced part-skim mozzarella cheese
4 large pieces roasted sweet red pepper, patted dry
12 fresh basil leaves
1/2 cup chopped pitted green olives

Cut the top half off the loaf of bread; carefully hollow out top and bottom, leaving a 3/4-in. shell (save removed bread for another use).

In a small bowl, combine lemon peel and 2 tablespoons oil. Spread over the cut side of bread top. Drizzle remaining oil inside bread bottom; layer with cheese, red pepper, basil and olives. Replace bread top. Wrap in foil. Bake at 350° for 10-12 minutes or until cheese is melted. Slice before serving. **Yield:** 4 servings.

This hot, robust sandwich features fresh basil leaves, tangy olives, roasted red pepper and melted mozzarella cheese.
—Taste of Home
Test Kitchen

Refried Bean Soup 30

prep/total time: 30 min.

1 can (28 ounces) crushed tomatoes
1/2 cup chopped onion
1/2 teaspoon minced garlic
1 can (31 ounces) refried beans
1 can (14-1/2 ounces) chicken broth
1 tablespoon minced fresh cilantro
5 corn tortillas (6 inches), cut into 1/2-inch strips, optional

In a large saucepan, bring the tomatoes, onion and garlic to a boil. Reduce heat; simmer, uncovered, for 5 minutes. Stir in the refried beans, broth and cilantro; simmer for 15 minutes.

Meanwhile, if tortilla strips are desired, place strips on a baking sheet. Bake at 350° for 12-15 minutes or until crisp. Garnish soup with tortilla strips. **Yield:** 8 servings (2 quarts).

Hearty servings of this soup are always welcome in my home. It's very quick and easy to put together, and you can add any garnishes you like. My husband and I love the flavor of this yummy soup. —Barbara Dean Littleton, Colorado

(tip) **Tasty Toppings:** Try topping off bowlfuls of this soup with sour cream and shredded Monterey Jack cheese.

20 Onion Soup with Sausage

prep/total time: 20 min.

1/2 **pound pork sausage links, cut into 1/2-inch pieces**
1 **pound sliced fresh mushrooms**
1 **cup sliced onion**
2 **cans (14-1/2 ounces *each*) beef broth**
4 **slices Italian bread**
1/2 **cup shredded part-skim mozzarella cheese**

In a large saucepan, cook sausage over medium heat until no longer pink; drain. Add mushrooms and onion; cook for 4-6 minutes or until tender. Stir in the broth. Bring to a boil. Reduce heat; simmer, uncovered, for 4-6 minutes or until heated through.

Ladle soup into four 2-cup ovenproof bowls. Top each with a slice of bread; sprinkle with cheese. Broil until cheese is melted. **Yield:** 4 servings.

With broiled mozzarella cheese bread on top, bowls of this savory soup make an impressive lunch or supper. It's ready in no time and is excellent in both taste and presentation.
—*Sundra Hauck*
Bogalusa, Louisiana

Broth Substitutions: (tip) Don't have canned broth? Follow instructions for dissolving beef bouillon cubes or granules in boiling water to make an equivalent amount of broth.

South-of-the-Border Chowder

prep/total time: 20 min.

- 1/2 cup chopped onion
- 4 bacon strips, diced
- 2 tablespoons all-purpose flour
- 1/2 teaspoon ground cumin
- 1/2 teaspoon chili powder
- 1/8 teaspoon garlic powder
- 1 package (32 ounces) frozen Southern-style hash brown potatoes
- 2 cans (14-1/2 ounces *each*) chicken broth
- 1 can (14-3/4 ounces) cream-style corn
- 1 can (11 ounces) Mexicorn, drained
- 1 can (4 ounces) chopped green chilies
- 1/4 cup pearl onions

Sour cream and minced fresh cilantro, optional

In a Dutch oven or soup kettle, saute onion and bacon until onion is tender and bacon is crisp. Stir in the flour, cumin, chili powder and garlic powder. Bring to a boil; cook and stir for 1 minute or until thickened.

Stir in the hash browns, broth, cream corn, Mexicorn, chilies and pearl onions. Bring to a boil. Reduce heat; simmer, uncovered, for 10 minutes or until heated through. Garnish with sour cream and cilantro if desired. **Yield:** 10 servings (2-1/2 quarts).

Loaded with potatoes, sweet corn, pearl onions and smoky bacon, this fast, filling chowder has a satisfying Southwestern flavor. —Tonya Burkhard Port Charlotte, Florida

10 Tuna Cheese Sandwiches

prep/total time: 10 min.

- 1 can (6 ounces) tuna, drained, flaked
- 1 cup (4 ounces) shredded cheddar cheese
- 1/2 cup chopped walnuts
- 1/2 cup mayonnaise
- 1 tablespoon milk
- 1 teaspoon lemon juice
- 1/2 teaspoon Worcestershire sauce
- 1/4 teaspoon onion salt
- 1/8 teaspoon pepper
- 10 slices whole wheat bread
- 2-1/2 cups finely shredded lettuce

In a small bowl, combine the first nine ingredients. On five slices of bread, layer 1/2 cup lettuce and about 1/4 cup tuna mixture; top with remaining bread. **Yield:** 5 servings.

This is my husband Kent's very favorite sandwich, so I make it often. —Barbara Billeter, Clovis, California

30 Cheddar Ham Soup

prep/total time: 30 min.

2 cups diced peeled potatoes
2 cups water
1/2 cup sliced carrot
1/4 cup chopped onion
1/4 cup butter, cubed
1/4 cup all-purpose flour
2 cups milk
1/4 to 1/2 teaspoon salt
1/4 teaspoon pepper
2 cups (8 ounces) shredded cheddar cheese
1-1/2 cups cubed fully cooked ham
1 cup frozen peas, thawed

In a large saucepan, combine the potatoes, water, carrot and onion. Bring to a boil. Reduce heat; cover and cook for 10-15 minutes or until tender.

Meanwhile, in another saucepan, melt butter. Stir in flour until smooth. Gradually add the milk, salt and pepper. Bring to a boil; cook and stir for 2 minutes or until thickened. Stir in the cheese until melted. Stir into undrained potato mixture. Add ham and peas; heat through. **Yield:** 7 servings.

I knew this thick soup was a keeper when my mother-in-law asked for the recipe! Chock-full of ham, veggies and cheese, it's creamy and comforting.
—Marty Matthews
Clarksville, Tennessee

Toasted Zippy Beef Sandwiches 20

prep/total time: 20 min.

1/4 cup mayonnaise
4-1/2 teaspoons Western salad dressing
1 tablespoon prepared horseradish
4 whole wheat sandwich buns, split
1/2 pound sliced deli roast beef
4 slices provolone cheese
4 slices Swiss cheese
4 slices tomato
4 slices onion
1 small sweet yellow pepper, sliced
4 large lettuce leaves

In a small bowl, combine the mayonnaise, salad dressing and horseradish; set aside. Place bun bottoms cut side up on an ungreased baking sheet; top with beef and cheeses. Broil 4 in. from the heat for 4-5 minutes or until cheese is melted.

Place bun tops cut side up on another baking sheet. Broil for 1-2 minutes or until golden brown. Meanwhile, layer the tomato, onion, yellow pepper and lettuce on sandwiches. Spread mayonnaise mixture over bun tops; place over lettuce. **Yield:** 4 sandwiches.

These sandwiches taste like they came from a delicatessen. With roast beef, two kinds of cheese, fresh veggies and a simple homemade dressing, they're comforting yet have a slight kick.
—Theresa Young
McHenry, Illinois

tip **Perfect Pairing:** These roast beef sandwiches and a colorful pasta salad from the deli make a casual weeknight meal, but they're festive enough to serve at any warm-weather gathering.

⏲20 Supper Sandwiches

prep/total time: 20 min.

1/2	pound fully cooked kielbasa *or* Polish sausage
1/2	medium sweet red pepper, julienned
1	small onion, halved and thinly sliced
1-1/2	teaspoons butter
1/2	cup chopped tomato, optional
1	to 2 tablespoons mustard *or* mayonnaise
2	hoagie buns, split and toasted

Cut sausage in half widthwise; cut each piece lengthwise to within 1/4 in. of opposite side. Place sausage cut side down in a large skillet; add red pepper, onion and butter. Cook over medium-high heat until vegetables are tender. Add tomato if desired; heat through. Spread mustard over cut sides of buns; fill with sausage and vegetables. **Yield:** 2 servings.

Come summertime, all entrees should be as easy as these hefty and flavorful sandwiches!
—Esther Danielson
Lake Arrowhead, California

- - - - - - - - - - - - - - - - -

Make Your Own Spread: Mix 2 tablespoons each mayonnaise and finely chopped oil-packed sun-dried tomatoes with 2 teaspoons minced red onion. Use in place of the mustard or plain mayonnaise.

tip

⏱ Speedy Seafood Gumbo

prep/total time: 15 min.

- 3 cups water, *divided*
- 1 tablespoon butter
- 1/4 teaspoon salt
- 1 cup uncooked instant rice
- 4 cans (10-3/4 ounces *each*) condensed chicken gumbo soup, undiluted
- 1 pound frozen cooked shrimp, peeled and deveined
- 1 package (10 ounces) frozen cut okra
- 1 package (8 ounces) imitation crabmeat, flaked
- 1 tablespoon dried minced onion
- 1 teaspoon Cajun seasoning
- 1/2 teaspoon garlic powder

In a small saucepan, bring 1 cup of water, butter and salt to a boil. Stir in rice; cover and remove from the heat. Let stand for 5 minutes.

Meanwhile, in a Dutch oven or soup kettle, combine the soup, shrimp, okra, crab, onion, Cajun seasoning, garlic powder and remaining water. Bring to a boil. Reduce heat; cover and cook over medium heat until heated through. Stir in cooked rice. **Yield:** 12 servings (3 quarts).

I needed a quick meal one blustery night when my husband was coming home late with the kids. So I threw together this tasty gumbo with ingredients I had on hand, and my family really liked it.
—*Lori Costo, The Woodlands, Texas*

⏱30 Veggie Bean Soup

prep/total time: 25 min.

- 1/2 cup chopped onion
- 1/2 cup sliced celery
- 1/2 cup sliced fresh carrots
- 1/2 teaspoon minced garlic
- 1 tablespoon olive oil
- 2 cups water
- 1 can (15-1/2 ounces) great northern beans, rinsed and drained
- 3/4 cup chicken broth
- 3/4 cup Italian stewed tomatoes
- 1/2 cup cubed peeled potato
- 1/2 cup frozen cut green beans
- 1 bay leaf
- 1/2 teaspoon salt
- 1/4 teaspoon pepper

In a large saucepan, saute onion, celery, carrots and garlic in oil until tender. Stir in remaining ingredients. Bring to a boil. Reduce heat; simmer, uncovered, for 15 minutes or until heated through. Discard bay leaf. **Yield:** 4 servings.

As chairman of the kitchen at my church, I wanted a meatless soup for a Lenten lunch. I came up with this colorful blend of vegetables, and received rave reviews.
—*Lois Dean, Williamson, West Virginia*

30 Speedy Weeknight Chili

prep/total time: 30 min.

1-1/2 pounds ground beef
2 small onions, chopped
1/2 cup chopped green pepper
1 teaspoon minced garlic
2 cans (16 ounces *each*) kidney beans, rinsed and drained
2 cans (14-1/2 ounces *each*) stewed tomatoes
1 can (28 ounces) crushed tomatoes
1 bottle (12 ounces) beer *or* nonalcoholic beer
1 can (6 ounces) tomato paste

1/4 cup chili powder
3/4 teaspoon dried oregano
1/2 teaspoon hot pepper sauce
1/4 teaspoon sugar
1/4 teaspoon salt
1/4 teaspoon pepper

In a large saucepan or Dutch oven, cook the beef, onions, green pepper and garlic over medium heat until meat is no longer pink; drain. Add remaining ingredients; bring to a boil. Reduce heat; simmer, uncovered, for 10 minutes. **Yield:** 15 servings.

Super-easy and great-tasting, this chili is so quick to cook. I use my food processor to chop up the veggies and cut down on prep time. It's also very tasty and lower in fat when made with ground turkey breast.
—Cynthia Hudson
Greenville, South Carolina

Sensational Sloppy Joes 30

prep/total time: 30 min.

1 **pound ground beef**
1/2 **cup chopped onion**
1/2 **cup condensed tomato soup**
1/2 **cup ketchup**
3 **tablespoons grape jelly**
1 **tablespoon brown sugar**
1 **tablespoon cider vinegar**
1 **tablespoon prepared mustard**
1/2 **teaspoon salt**
1/2 **teaspoon celery seed**
5 **hamburger buns, split**

In a large skillet, cook beef and onion over medium heat until meat is no longer pink; drain. Stir in the soup, ketchup, jelly, brown sugar, vinegar, mustard, salt and celery seed. Bring to a boil. Reduce heat; simmer, uncovered, for 10 minutes or until heated through. Serve on buns. **Yield:** 5 servings.

I've always liked sloppy joes but was feeling that my own recipe lacked character. Then a co-worker shared hers, and I guarantee I'll never go back! —Jessica Mergen Cuba City, Wisconsin

 Sweet Ingredient: Grape jelly adds a hint of sweetness to these flavorful sandwiches. If you'd like them extra-sweet, use more than called for.

⏱30 Stuffed Pepper Soup

prep/total time: 30 min.

1 pouch (8.8 ounces) ready-to-serve long grain and wild rice
1 pound ground beef
2 cups frozen chopped green peppers, thawed
1 cup chopped onions
1 jar (26 ounces) chunky tomato pasta sauce
1 can (14-1/2 ounces) Italian diced tomatoes, undrained
1 can (14 ounces) beef broth

Prepare rice according to package directions. Meanwhile, in a large saucepan, cook the beef, green peppers and onions until meat is no longer pink; drain. Stir in the pasta sauce, tomatoes, broth and prepared rice; heat through. **Yield:** 6-8 servings (about 2 quarts).

This is an excellent example of how convenience foods can be combined to make a tasty entree. Ready in minutes when I get home from work, this soup is part of a balanced meal with a tossed salad, rolls or fruit. For variety, try ground chicken, turkey or even venison instead of ground beef.
—Tracy Thompson
Cranesville, Pennsylvania

Pepper Steak Sandwiches

prep/total time: 25 min.

- 1 pound frozen beef sandwich steaks, thawed
- 4 teaspoons vegetable oil, *divided*
- 1 medium sweet onion, chopped
- 3/4 cup julienned green pepper
- 1/4 teaspoon salt
- 1/4 teaspoon pepper
- 1 cup chopped dill pickles
- 1/2 cup Italian salad dressing
- 1/2 cup chopped fresh tomato
- 1/4 cup chopped red onion
- 5 hard rolls, split
- 2 cups (8 ounces) shredded part-skim mozzarella cheese

In a large skillet, cook steaks in 2 teaspoons oil in batches over medium heat for 3-4 minutes or until no longer pink. Meanwhile, in another skillet, saute the sweet onion and green pepper in remaining oil until tender; sprinkle with salt and pepper.

In a small bowl, combine the pickles, salad dressing, tomato and red onion; set aside.

Place the roll tops cut side up on a baking sheet. Sprinkle with cheese. Broil 4 in. from the heat for 2 minutes or until cheese is melted. Divide steaks among roll bottoms; top with onion mixture and pickle mixture. Replace roll tops. **Yield:** 5 servings.

My husband came up with these sandwiches years ago, when we had just started dating. He fixed them for my family, and we were hooked. They're still a favorite to this day. —Julie Tullos, Clinton, Mississippi

----

(tip) **Sandwich Tips:**
Instead of sandwich steaks, use a pound of rib eye steak sliced as paper-thin as the butcher can get it. Make the pickle topping the day before because the longer it sits, the better it gets.

Club Sandwiches

prep/total time: 25 min.

- 1/2 cup mayonnaise
- 4 French rolls, split
- 1 cup shredded lettuce
- 8 slices tomato
- 1 medium ripe avocado, peeled and sliced
- 1/4 cup prepared Italian salad dressing
- 1/2 teaspoon coarsely ground pepper
- 12 cooked bacon strips
- 1/2 pound sliced deli turkey
- 1/2 pound sliced deli ham
- 4 slices Swiss cheese

Spread mayonnaise over cut sides of rolls. On roll bottoms, layer lettuce, tomato and avocado. Drizzle with dressing; sprinkle with pepper. Layer with bacon, turkey, ham and cheese. Replace roll tops. **Yield:** 4 servings.

I'm a busy wife, mother, grandmother and great-grandmother. One of our favorite sandwiches is what we call "hunka munka"...and it's a complete meal.
—Janet Miller, Midland, Texas

⑩ Deli Monte Cristos

prep/total time: 10 min.

- 4 slices rye bread
- 4 thin slices deli ham
- 2 thin slices deli turkey
- 2 tablespoons deli coleslaw
- 2 tablespoons Thousand Island salad dressing
- 2 slices Swiss cheese
- 2 eggs

On two slices of bread, layer a slice of ham and turkey, coleslaw, salad dressing and cheese. Top with remaining ham and bread. In a shallow bowl, whisk the eggs. Dip both sides of sandwiches in eggs.

In a nonstick skillet coated with nonstick cooking spray, cook sandwiches over medium heat for 2-3 minutes on each side or until bread is toasted and cheese is melted. **Yield:** 2 servings.

Looking for a change from the typical Reuben or grilled cheese? This was a famous sandwich in the islands years ago. We make it often, and I always get requests for more.
—Darlene Van Wie Clayton, New York

Zesty Potato Cheese Soup ⏱⑩

prep/total time: 10 min.

3 cans (10-3/4 ounces *each*) condensed cream of potato soup, undiluted

2 cans (12 ounces *each*) evaporated milk

3/4 cup shredded cheddar cheese

3/4 cup shredded pepper Jack cheese

6 slices ready-to-serve fully cooked bacon, crumbled

In a large saucepan, combine the potato soup and milk. Cook over medium heat for 5-7 minutes or until heated through. Ladle into serving bowls. Sprinkle with cheeses and bacon. **Yield:** 6 servings.

I really like to make potato cheese soup from scratch. But one night, we were in a hurry, so I added a few ingredients to canned potato soup instead. It was so good that now I always keep a few cans on hand...it's so quick and easy!
—Karen Pigmon
Corning, California

(tip) **Add More Zip:** If you like your soup even zestier, stir in some chopped green chilies to suit your taste.

⏱ Turkey Meatball Soup

prep/total time: 30 min.

3 cups cut fresh green beans
2 cups fresh baby carrots
2 cups chicken broth
1 teaspoon dried oregano
1 teaspoon dried basil
1 teaspoon minced garlic
2 cans (14-1/2 ounces *each*) Italian stewed tomatoes
1 package (12 ounces) refrigerated fully cooked Italian turkey meatballs
2 cups frozen corn

In a large saucepan or soup kettle, combine the first six ingredients. Bring to a boil. Reduce heat; cover and simmer for 10 minutes. Add the tomatoes, meatballs and corn. Cover and cook over medium-low heat for 10 minutes or until the meatballs are heated through. **Yield:** 6 servings.

We combined ready-made turkey meatballs with fresh and frozen vegetables to come up with this nicely seasoned soup.
—Taste of Home Test Kitchen

- - - - - - - - - - - - - - -

Freeze Some or Double It: Small families can enjoy half of this soup now and freeze the rest for later. But bigger families may want to double the recipe, so there will be plenty left over for a second meal. **tip**

Sausage Bean Soup

prep/total time: 30 min.

    4 cups water
    1 medium potato, peeled and chopped
    6 brown-and-serve turkey sausage links
       (1 ounce *each*)
    2 cans (16 ounces *each*) kidney beans,
       rinsed and drained
    1 can (28 ounces) diced tomatoes,
       undrained
    1 cup chopped onion
    1 medium green pepper, chopped
    1 bay leaf
  1/2 teaspoon *each* garlic salt,
       seasoned salt, pepper and dried
       thyme

In a large saucepan, bring water and potato to a boil. Cover and cook for 10-15 minutes or until tender (do not drain). Meanwhile, crumble sausage into a skillet; cook over medium heat until browned. Drain if necessary. Add to saucepan.

Stir in the remaining ingredients. Bring to a boil. Reduce heat; simmer, uncovered, for 8-10 minutes or until heated through, stirring occasionally. Discard bay leaf. **Yield:** 10 servings.

This soup is so simple to assemble with ingredients that are easy to keep on hand, and it's delicious to boot. —Gail Wilkerson, House Springs, Missouri

Curry Chicken Salad Wraps

prep/total time: 25 min.

  1/2 cup mayonnaise
  1/2 cup sour cream
  1/4 cup finely chopped green onions
    2 tablespoons curry powder
    1 tablespoon mango chutney
  1/2 teaspoon salt
  1/2 teaspoon pepper
    1 package (10 ounces) ready-to-serve
       roasted chicken breast strips
    1 cup seedless red grapes, halved
  1/2 cup julienned carrot
    6 tablespoons chopped pecans, toasted
  1/4 cup thinly sliced onion
    6 lettuce leaves
    6 flour tortillas (10 inches), warmed
  3/4 cup fresh mint (about 24 leaves)

For dressing, in a small bowl, combine first seven ingredients. Set aside 1-1/2 cups for serving. In a large bowl, combine the chicken, grapes, carrot, pecans and onion. Stir in remaining dressing.

Place a lettuce leaf on each tortilla; top each with 2/3 cup chicken salad and mint leaves. Roll up. Serve with reserved dressing. **Yield:** 6 servings.

With curry powder and mango chutney, these sandwiches offer a twist on traditional chicken salad. —Robyn Cavallaro, Easton, Pennsylvania

⓴ Grilled Ham 'n' Jack Cheese

prep/total time: 15 min.

4 tablespoons butter, softened
8 slices Texas toast
4 slices sharp cheddar cheese
16 thin slices deli ham
4 slices red onion, optional
4 tablespoons ranch salad dressing
4 slices pepper Jack cheese

Butter one side of each slice of Texas toast. On the unbuttered sides of four slices, layer cheddar cheese, half of the ham, onion if desired and remaining ham; spread with ranch dressing. Top with pepper Jack cheese and remaining toast, buttered side up.

On a hot griddle, cook sandwiches for 3-4 minutes or until bottoms of sandwiches are browned. Carefully turn; cook 2 minutes longer or until cheese is melted. **Yield:** 4 servings.

Make your family these sandwiches for supper, and you have the kind of comfort food that's the stuff of childhood memories. They're fast, filling and nice enough to serve company.
—Jayne Ward
Eldon, Missouri

- - - - - - - - - - - - - - -

Serving
Suggestion:
Pop some fries in the oven to serve with these sandwiches. Rootbeer or cola floats would be a sweet way to round out this all-American meal.

tip

Beef Soup in a Hurry ⑩

prep/total time: 10 min.

1 can (24 ounces) beef stew
1 can (14-1/2 ounces) stewed tomatoes, cut up
1 can (10-3/4 ounces) condensed vegetable beef soup, undiluted
1 can (8-3/4 ounces) whole kernel corn, drained
1/8 teaspoon hot pepper sauce

Combine all ingredients in a microwave-safe bowl. Cover and microwave on high for 2-3 minutes or until heated through, stirring once. **Yield:** 6 servings.

Editor's Note: This recipe was tested in a 1,100-watt microwave.

I need just a few pantry goods to stir up this comforting microwave mixture. I call this "throw-together soup."
—Loellen Holley
Topock, Arizona

30 Vegetarian White Bean Soup

prep/total time: 30 min.

2 small zucchini, quartered
  lengthwise and sliced
1 cup *each* chopped onion, celery
  and carrot
2 tablespoons canola oil
3 cans (14-1/2 ounces *each*)
  vegetable broth
1 can (15-1/2 ounces) great
  northern beans, rinsed and
  drained
1 can (15 ounces) white kidney *or*
  cannellini beans, rinsed and
  drained

1 can (14-1/2 ounces) diced
  tomatoes, undrained
1/2 teaspoon dried thyme
1/2 teaspoon dried oregano
1/4 teaspoon pepper

In a large saucepan or Dutch oven, saute the zucchini, onion, celery and carrot in oil for 5-7 minutes or until crisp-tender. Add the remaining ingredients. Bring to a boil. Reduce heat; cover and simmer for 15 minutes or until vegetables are tender. **Yield:** 7 servings.

Hearty with two kinds of beans, this fresh-tasting, meatless soup makes a satisfying entree that's good for you, too.
—*Taste of Home Test Kitchen*

Picking Out Zucchini: (tip) When buying zucchini, look for smaller squash with glossy, smooth and firm skins.

Stuffed Sourdough Sandwiches ③⓪

prep/total time: 30 min.

1-1/2 **pounds ground beef**
1/2 **cup chopped onion**
1 **can (15 ounces) tomato sauce**
1 **can (4 ounces) chopped green chilies**
1/2 **cup chopped fresh mushrooms**
2 **tablespoons chili powder**
2 **tablespoons sliced ripe olives**
1/4 **teaspoon garlic salt**
1 **cup (4 ounces) shredded cheddar cheese**
8 **sourdough rolls**

In a large skillet, cook beef and onion over medium heat until meat is no longer pink; drain. Add the tomato sauce, chilies, mushrooms, chili powder, olives and garlic salt. Bring to a boil. Reduce heat; simmer, uncovered, for 10 minutes or until heated through. Add cheese; cook and stir until melted.

Cut 1/4 in. off the top of each roll; set aside. Carefully hollow out bottom of each roll, leaving a 1/4-in. shell (discard removed bread or save for another use). Fill each roll with about 1/2 cup meat mixture. Replace bread tops.

Individually wrap four sandwiches tightly in foil; freeze for up to 3 months. Place remaining sandwiches on a baking sheet. Bake at 350° for 10-15 minutes or until heated through.

To use frozen sandwiches: Thaw in the refrigerator overnight. Place foil-wrapped sandwiches on baking sheets. Bake at 350° for 20-25 minutes or until heated through.
Yield: 8 servings.

These delicious stuffed sandwiches are easy to put together. Some can be baked as soon as they're assembled, while the rest can be frozen for a quick dinner later.
—Shannon Hansen
Oxnard, California

(20) Crab Patties

prep/total time: 20 min.

1 egg, lightly beaten
1/4 cup dry bread crumbs
2 tablespoons finely chopped onion
1-1/2 teaspoons prepared horseradish
1-1/2 teaspoons chopped sweet red pepper
1-1/2 teaspoons Dijon mustard
1/8 teaspoon salt
1/8 teaspoon cayenne pepper
1/4 cup mayonnaise, *divided*
6 ounces imitation crabmeat, chopped
1 tablespoon butter
2 English muffins, split and toasted
4 slices tomato
1/2 cup shredded Swiss cheese

In a large bowl, combine the first eight ingredients; stir in 2 tablespoons mayonnaise. Add crab and mix well. Shape into four patties. In a large skillet, cook patties in butter over medium heat for 3-4 minutes on each side or until golden brown.

Place the English muffins on a baking sheet. Spread with remaining mayonnaise. Top with tomato, crab patties and cheese. Broil 4 in. from the heat for 2 minutes or until cheese is melted. **Yield:** 4 servings.

I've been whipping up batches of these delicious patties for years. They're always a hit, whether I serve them for brunch, lunch or a quick dinner to friends, family or even the grandkids.
—Paula Marchesi
Lenhartsville,
Pennsylvania

(tip)

Other Options: Instead of crab, you can use canned tuna or salmon to make these patties. And you can substitute kaiser rolls for the English muffins.

Vegetable Beef Soup 30

prep/total time: 30 min.

4 cups cubed peeled potatoes
6 cups water
1 pound ground beef
5 teaspoons beef bouillon granules
1 can (10-3/4 ounces) condensed tomato soup, undiluted
2 cups frozen corn, thawed
2 cups frozen sliced carrots, thawed
2 cups frozen cut green beans, thawed
2 cups frozen sliced okra, thawed
3 tablespoons dried minced onion

In a Dutch oven or soup kettle, bring potatoes and water to a boil. Cover and cook for 10-15 minutes or until tender. Meanwhile, in a large skillet, cook beef over medium heat until no longer pink; drain.

Add the bouillon, soup, vegetables, dried minced onion and beef to the undrained potatoes. Reduce heat; simmer, uncovered, for 8-10 minutes or until heated through, stirring occasionally. **Yield:** 14 servings (3-1/2 quarts).

Just brimming with veggies, this hearty soup will warm family and friends right down to their toes!
—Marie Carlisle
Sumrall, Mississippi

⏱30 Spicy Cheeseburgers

prep/total time: 30 min.

1 small onion, finely chopped
2 teaspoons minced garlic
2 teaspoons Worcestershire sauce
2 teaspoons Liquid Smoke, optional
1 teaspoon lemon-pepper seasoning
1 teaspoon pepper
1/2 teaspoon salt
1/2 teaspoon ground mustard
1/2 teaspoon cayenne pepper
1/2 teaspoon lemon juice
3 pounds ground beef
9 slices pepper Jack cheese
9 hamburger buns, split
Lettuce leaves and tomato slices, optional

In a large bowl, combine the first 10 ingredients. Crumble beef over mixture and mix well. Shape into nine patties.

Grill, uncovered, over medium heat for 7-8 minutes on each side or until no longer pink. Top with cheese. Grill 3-5 minutes longer or until cheese is melted. Serve on buns with lettuce and tomato if desired. **Yield:** 9 servings.

We think this is the best burger recipe ever! The burgers are both flavorful and filling. For extra kick, we added cayenne pepper to the ground beef, then topped the patties with pepper Jack cheese.
—Jonna Tuchscherer
Bellevue, Washington

Spinach Turkey Burgers 20

prep/total time: 20 min.

1 cup stuffing mix, finely crushed
1/3 cup chicken broth
1/2 teaspoon Italian seasoning
1/4 teaspoon salt
1/4 teaspoon pepper
1 package (10 ounces) frozen chopped spinach, thawed and squeezed dry
1 pound ground turkey
4 sandwich buns, split
Cheese slices, lettuce leaves and tomato slices, optional

In a large bowl, combine the stuffing mix, broth, Italian seasoning, salt, pepper and half of the spinach (save remaining spinach for another use). Crumble turkey over mixture and mix well. Shape into four 3/4-in.-thick patties.

Grill, uncovered, over medium-hot heat or broil 3-4 in. from the heat for 3-4 minutes on each side or until juices run clear. Serve on buns with cheese, lettuce and tomato if desired. **Yield:** 4 servings.

If you're looking for a change-of-pace burger, try these easy sandwiches. Instead of beef, the patties are made with ground turkey, spinach and stuffing mix for a tasty twist on the usual grilled fare.
—C.A. Hedges
Clarence Center, New York

(tip) **Doneness Test:** Cook beef, pork and lamb burgers to 160°; cook chicken or turkey burgers to 165°. Insert an instant-read thermometer from the side of the burger.

⏱30 Basil Burgers

prep/total time: 25 min.

2 tablespoons minced fresh basil
or 2 teaspoons dried basil
1 tablespoon olive oil
1/2 teaspoon minced garlic
1/2 teaspoon salt
1/2 teaspoon pepper
1-1/2 pounds ground beef
1/4 cup cream cheese, softened
4 onion rolls, split and toasted
4 slices red onion
1 medium ripe avocado, peeled and sliced

In a bowl, combine first five ingredients. Crumble beef over mixture and mix well. Shape into four patties.

Grill, uncovered, over medium-hot heat for 5-7 minutes on each side or until juices run clear. Spread cream cheese over cut side of roll tops. Place burgers, onion and avocado on the roll bottoms; replace the tops. **Yield:** 4 servings.

We've been making these burgers for years. Served on onion rolls with cream cheese and avocado, they're a refreshing change from the regular cheeseburger. Everybody asks for them.
—Jill Christopher
Grants Pass, Oregon

Cantonese Chicken Burgers 30

prep/total time: 30 min.

1 egg
1 teaspoon sesame oil
1 teaspoon soy sauce
1/3 cup dry bread crumbs
1/4 cup chopped salted peanuts
2 tablespoons sliced green onion
2 tablespoons shredded carrot
1/8 teaspoon garlic powder
1 pound ground chicken
4 hamburger buns, split and toasted
1/2 cup plum sauce
8 spinach leaves, chopped

In a large bowl, whisk the egg, oil and soy sauce. Stir in the bread crumbs, peanuts, onion, carrot and garlic powder. Crumble chicken over mixture and mix well. Shape into four patties.

Grill, uncovered, over medium-hot heat or broil 3-4 in. from the heat for 8-10 minutes on each side or until juices run clear. Serve on buns, topped with plum sauce and spinach. **Yield:** 4 servings.

Ground chicken is perked up with sesame oil, soy sauce, green onion and chopped peanuts to make these delectably different burgers. These sandwiches may take a bit more work than the regular burger, but the taste is worth it.
—Betty Carr
Huntsville, Ohio

(tip) **Don't Lose the Juice:** Don't use a spatula to flatten burgers while cooking—you'll squeeze out the succulent juices.

30 Tex-Mex Turkey Burgers

prep/total time: 25 min.

1-1/4 pounds ground turkey
1 envelope reduced-sodium taco seasoning
1 tablespoon dried cilantro flakes
1 cup (4 ounces) shredded Mexican cheese blend
1/2 cup sour cream
1/2 cup salsa
4 hamburger buns, split
4 lettuce leaves

In a large bowl, combine the turkey, taco seasoning and cilantro; shape into four patties. Grill, covered, over medium heat or broil 4-6 in. from the heat for 5 minutes on each side.

Sprinkle cheese over burgers; grill 2-3 minutes longer or until a meat thermometer reads 165° and cheese is melted. Combine sour cream and salsa. Serve burgers on buns with sour cream mixture and lettuce. **Yield:** 4 servings.

Flavored with taco seasoning and cilantro, these Southwestern turkey burgers are so good. I top them with a mixture of salsa and sour cream instead of ketchup.
—Nancy Bourget
Round Rock, Texas

Toasting Hamburger Buns: Simply butter both sides of the buns; place butter-side down on the grill for about 5 minutes or until golden brown.

(tip)

salads & sides

30 Crunchy Romaine Strawberry Salad

prep/total time: 30 min.

1 package (3 ounces) ramen noodles
1 cup chopped walnuts
1/4 cup butter
1/4 cup vegetable oil
1/4 cup sugar
2 tablespoons red wine vinegar
1/2 teaspoon soy sauce
8 cups torn romaine
1/2 cup chopped green onions
2 cups fresh strawberries, sliced

Discard seasoning packet from ramen noodles or save for another use. Break noodles into small pieces. In a skillet, saute noodles and walnuts in butter for 8-10 minutes or until golden; cool.

For dressing, in a jar with a tight-fitting lid, combine the oil, sugar, vinegar and soy sauce; shake well. Just before serving, combine the romaine, onions, strawberries and noodle mixture in a large bowl. Drizzle with dressing and toss gently. **Yield:** 12 servings.

This is such an impressive salad. It's been a hit at every get-together we've attended. In addition to being pretty and colorful, it's so easy to make. And the mouth-watering combination of tastes and textures seems to please every palate.
—Leslie Lancaster
Zachary, Louisiana

Chicken-Stuffed Tomatoes 20

prep/total time: 20 min.

4 medium tomatoes
1 cooked rotisserie chicken, skin removed and cubed (2-3/4 cups)
1/2 cup shredded carrot
1/4 cup chopped green onions
1/3 cup mayonnaise
1/3 cup ranch salad dressing
1/4 cup chopped walnuts

Cut a thin slice off the top of each tomato. Scoop out pulp, leaving 1/2-in. shells. Invert tomatoes onto paper towels to drain.

In a small bowl, combine the chicken, carrot and onions. Combine mayonnaise and ranch dressing; stir into chicken mixture. Spoon into tomatoes. Sprinkle with walnuts. **Yield:** 4 servings.

I turn garden-fresh tomatoes into a sensational summer meal when I fill them with this creamy chicken salad. I came up with this recipe when I had a lot of fresh tomatoes on hand.
—Nancy MacLeod
Boynton Beach, Florida

(tip) **Storing Tomatoes:** Keep unwashed tomatoes at room temperature until ripe. Store out of direct sunlight. Tomatoes can be kept in the fridge up to 3 days.

(30) Cider-Glazed Carrots

prep/total time: 30 min.

3 cups julienned fresh carrots
2 tablespoons butter
1 tablespoon brown sugar
1/2 cup apple cider *or* juice
3 tablespoons water
1 teaspoon Dijon mustard

In a large skillet, saute carrots in butter for 5 minutes. Add brown sugar. Cook and stir for 1 minute or until the sugar is dissolved.

Stir in the cider, water and mustard. Bring to a boil. Reduce heat; cover and simmer for 10-12 minutes or until carrots are crisp-tender. Uncover and cook 3 minutes longer. Stir to coat carrots with the glaze. **Yield:** 4 servings.

You'll find that these sweet carrots taste great served alongside any main dish.
—Taste of Home Test Kitchen

- - - - - - - - - - - - - - - - - -

Time-Saving Tip: To make your preparation time quicker, use packaged shredded carrots. Then simply place all of the ingredients in a skillet and bring to a boil. Cover and simmer for 10-12 minutes. Uncover and cook 3 minutes longer or until the sauce is thickened.

Mushroom Rice

prep/total time: 25 min.

1 can (10-1/2 ounces) condensed beef broth, undiluted
3/4 cup uncooked long grain rice
1 jar (4-1/2 ounces) sliced mushrooms, undrained
1/4 cup butter, melted
1/2 teaspoon garlic powder
1/2 teaspoon onion salt

In a 2-qt. microwave-safe dish, combine all ingredients. Cover and microwave on high for 4 minutes. Microwave at 50% power for 12 minutes. Let stand for 5-10 minutes. Stir before serving. **Yield:** 4 servings.

Editor's Note: This recipe was tested in a 1,100-watt microwave.

A co-worker shared the recipe for this delicious rice side dish more than 30 years ago, and I've been taking it to potlucks ever since. It's a snap to throw together.
—Iris Hubbard
North Fort Myers, Florida

⏱20 Colorful Corn 'n' Bean Salad

prep/total time: 15 min.

1 can (15 ounces) black beans, rinsed and drained
1 jar (13 ounces) corn relish
1/2 cup canned kidney beans, rinsed and drained
1/2 cup quartered cherry tomatoes
1/2 cup chopped celery
1/4 cup chopped sweet orange pepper
1/4 cup sliced pimiento-stuffed olives
2 teaspoons minced fresh parsley

In a large bowl, combine all the ingredients. Cover and refrigerate until serving. **Yield:** 12 servings.

This quick recipe couldn't be easier...the liquid from the corn relish makes the fuss-free dressing! And because there's no mayo, it's a perfect salad to bring along on summer outings.
—TerryAnn Moore
Oaklyn, New Jersey

BLT Salad 30

prep/total time: 25 min.

1 pound sliced bacon, cut into 1-inch pieces
1/4 cup butter, cubed
4 slices white bread, crusts removed and cut into 1-inch cubes
1/2 cup mayonnaise
3 to 5 tablespoons minced fresh basil
2 tablespoons red wine vinegar
1/2 teaspoon pepper
1/2 teaspoon minced garlic
6 cups torn romaine
1-1/2 cups grape tomatoes

In a large skillet, cook bacon over medium heat until crisp. Using a slotted spoon, remove to paper towels; drain, reserving 2 tablespoons drippings. Set bacon and drippings aside. In another large skillet, melt butter. Add bread cubes; cook over medium heat for 4-5 minutes or until golden brown, stirring frequently. Remove to paper towels; cool.

For dressing, whisk the mayonnaise, basil, vinegar, pepper, garlic and reserved drippings. In a large bowl, combine romaine, tomatoes and bacon. Drizzle with dressing and toss to coat. Top with the croutons. **Yield:** 8 servings.

In my family of six, it's hard to find a vegetable or salad everyone will eat, but they all raved about this one. With basil from my garden, this salad is simple to make, but mouth-watering.
—Susie Clayton
South St. Paul, Minnesota

tip **Basil Basics:** Fresh basil turns black when stored in the refrigerator. Snip the ends and place the herb in a glass of water on your countertop.

(30) Cauliflower Tomato Medley

prep/total time: 30 min.

1	medium head cauliflower (about 2 pounds), broken into florets
6	bacon strips, diced
1-1/2	cups soft bread crumbs
3	medium tomatoes, cut into wedges
2	tablespoons sliced green onion
1-1/2	teaspoons snipped fresh dill or 1/2 teaspoon dill weed
1/4	teaspoon salt

Dash pepper

3/4 cup shredded cheddar cheese

Place cauliflower in a large saucepan; add 1 in. of water. Bring to a boil. Reduce heat; cover and simmer for 5-10 minutes or until crisp-tender.

Meanwhile, in a large skillet, cook bacon over medium heat until crisp. Using a slotted spoon, remove to paper towels. Drain, reserving 3 tablespoons drippings. Toss bacon and bread crumbs with drippings; set aside.

Drain cauliflower. Arrange the tomatoes in a greased shallow 2-qt. baking dish. Sprinkle with onion, dill, salt and pepper. Top with cauliflower and bacon mixture.

Cover and bake at 400° for 10 minutes. Uncover; sprinkle with cheese. Bake 5 minutes longer or until cheese is melted. **Yield:** 6 servings.

This dish is a great way to dress up a head of cauliflower and use up tomatoes. It goes nicely with most meat and fish entrees. —Lena Post St. Albert, Alberta

Freeze Fresh Dill: To enjoy fresh dill all winter, chop up the feathery leaves, freeze in small containers and pull off a pinch whenever needed to boost the flavor of potatoes, salads or soups.

(tip)

Short Thyme Broccoli
prep/total time: 15 min.

- 1/2 pound fresh broccoli florets
- 1 tablespoon olive oil
- 3/4 teaspoon lemon juice
- 1/8 teaspoon salt
- 1/8 teaspoon dried thyme

Place the broccoli and 1 in. of water in a saucepan; bring to a boil. Reduce heat; cover and simmer for 5-8 minutes or until crisp-tender. Meanwhile, in a small bowl, combine the oil, lemon juice, salt and thyme. Drain broccoli; toss with oil mixture. **Yield:** 4 servings.

Bottled lemon juice adds a splash of citrus to this simple treatment for fresh broccoli. Keep this recipe on hand; the versatile side dish will complement many main courses. —Taste of Home Test Kitchen

Seven-Fruit Salad
prep/total time: 10 min.

- 1 can (29 ounces) sliced peaches, drained
- 2 medium firm bananas, sliced
- 1 can (11 ounces) mandarin oranges, drained
- 1 cup sliced fresh strawberries
- 1 cup fresh *or* frozen blueberries
- 1 cup seedless grapes
- 1 jar (16 ounces) maraschino cherries, drained
- 1/3 cup corn syrup

In a large bowl, combine all of the ingredients. Serve with a slotted spoon. **Yield:** 10-12 servings.

This makes a great-tasting fruit salad that's speedy and pretty enough for any occasion.
—Nancy Zimmerman
Cape May Court House, New Jersey

20 Chili Cheese Corn
prep/total time: 15 min.

- 1 package (8 ounces) cream cheese, cubed
- 2 tablespoons butter
- 4 cups fresh *or* frozen corn, thawed
- 1 can (4 ounces) chopped green chilies
- 1/4 cup milk
- 1/4 teaspoon garlic salt
- 1/8 teaspoon salt
- 1/8 teaspoon cayenne pepper

In a large saucepan, combine cream cheese and butter. Cook and stir over medium heat for 4-5 minutes or until smooth. Stir in the remaining ingredients. Cook for 5 minutes or until heated through. Serve with a slotted spoon. **Yield:** 6 servings.

A co-worker shared this corn recipe more than 10 years ago. It's so easy and tasty that it's become a favorite in our family—especially for holidays or special meals. I've had many requests for the recipe.
—Nadene Melton, San Juan Capistrano, California

⑳ Crispy Crouton Salad

prep/total time: 20 min.

3 cups cubed Italian bread
3 medium tomatoes, chopped
6 ounces part-skim mozzarella cheese, cubed
1 medium sweet yellow pepper, cut into 1-inch pieces
1/3 cup minced fresh basil
6 tablespoons olive oil
3 tablespoons white *or* brown balsamic vinegar
1-1/2 teaspoons minced garlic
1/8 teaspoon salt
1/8 teaspoon pepper

Place bread cubes in a single layer in an ungreased 15-in. x 10-in. x 1-in. baking pan. Bake at 450° for 6-8 minutes or until golden brown, stirring twice. Cool.

In a large bowl, combine the tomatoes, mozzarella, yellow pepper and basil. In a jar with a tight-fitting lid, combine the oil, vinegar, garlic, salt and pepper; shake well. Drizzle over salad and toss to coat. Sprinkle with croutons. **Yield:** 8 servings.

Nothing says "summer" at our house like this unique salad! It's also a great way to use up basil and tomatoes from the garden. I've brought it to many women's luncheons at church because it's a much-requested favorite.
—LaNae Sanchez
Canyon Country, California

Smashed Red Potatoes 30

prep/total time: 25 min.

2   **pounds red potatoes, cut into small wedges**

1/4 **cup minced fresh parsley**

2   **tablespoons olive oil**

1   **teaspoon salt**

1/2 **teaspoon pepper**

Place the potatoes in a large saucepan and cover with water. Bring to a boil. Reduce heat to medium; cook, uncovered, for 15-20 minutes or until tender. Drain and place in a bowl. Coarsely mash the potatoes, adding the parsley, oil, salt and pepper. **Yield:** 6 servings.

Olive oil and parsley are a nice change from milk and butter in these mashed potatoes.
—*Taste of Home Test Kitchen*

(tip) **Red Potato Primer:** Good quality red potatoes will be firm, smooth-skinned and have bright red coloring. It's normal for them to have a few shallow "eyes." Stay away from red potatoes that are soft, wrinkled, green-tinted or that have cuts. Store red potatoes in a cool, dark, well-ventilated place for up to 2 weeks; do not refrigerate.

salads & sides

⑳ Dolloped Sweet Potatoes

prep/total time: 15 min.

4 small sweet potatoes
1 package (3 ounces) cream cheese, softened
1 tablespoon butter, softened
2 tablespoons brown sugar
1/4 teaspoon pumpkin pie spice

Scrub and pierce sweet potatoes; place on a microwave-safe plate. Microwave, uncovered, on high for 10-13 minutes or until tender, turning twice.

Meanwhile, in a small mixing bowl, beat the cream cheese, butter, brown sugar and pumpkin pie spice. Make a slice in the top of each potato; fluff pulp with a fork. Dollop with cream cheese mixture. **Yield:** 4 servings.

Editor's Note: This recipe was tested in a 1,100-watt microwave.

We used a little microwave magic to turn sweet potatoes into a speedy and special side dish for a holiday feast. Pumpkin pie spice and a hint of brown sugar flavor the rich cream cheese topping.
—*Taste of Home Test Kitchen*

Fruity Chicken Tossed Salad 🔟

prep/total time: 10 min.

12 cups Italian-blend salad greens
3 packages (6 ounces *each*)
   ready-to-serve grilled chicken
   breast strips
1 can (11 ounces) mandarin
   oranges, drained
1 cup seedless red grapes, halved
2/3 cup poppy seed salad dressing

In a large bowl, combine the salad greens, chicken, oranges and grapes. Drizzle with dressing and toss to coat. **Yield:** 6 servings.

This salad is a cinch to put together and always looks so pretty. For variety, try creamy cucumber salad dressing instead of poppy seed.
—Dee Drew
Aliso Viejo, California

Opt for Another Chicken: Try Southwestern-flavored chicken strips in place of the plain grilled ones. You could even heat them in a skillet just to take the chill off.

⏱️⃝20 Lemon-Pepper Vegetables

prep/total time: 20 min.

1 pound fresh green beans, trimmed and cut into 2-inch pieces
2 tablespoons water
1 small yellow summer squash, cut into 1/2-inch slices
1 cup halved cherry tomatoes
2 tablespoons butter
3/4 teaspoon lemon-pepper seasoning
1/4 teaspoon Italian seasoning

In a large microwave-safe bowl, combine the green beans and water. Cover and microwave on high for 5-6 minutes or until crisp-tender. Stir in squash. Cover and microwave on high for 2 minutes. Add tomatoes. Cover and cook 30 seconds longer or until heated through; drain. Gently stir in the butter, lemon-pepper and Italian seasoning. **Yield:** 6 servings.

Editor's Note: This recipe was tested in a 1,100-watt microwave.

This mildly seasoned side dish is sure to brighten up any dinner table!
—Taste of Home Test Kitchen

Handle With Care: (tip) Handle vegetables gently—they bruise easily, and a bruised spot will lead to decay.

Colorful Pasta Salad 20

prep/total time: 15 min.

1-1/2 cups uncooked tricolor spiral
pasta
1 can (8 ounces) unsweetened
pineapple chunks
1 cup fresh snow peas, halved
1/2 cup thinly sliced carrot
1/2 cup sliced cucumber
1 tablespoon minced fresh cilantro
1/4 cup Italian salad dressing

Cook pasta according to package directions. Meanwhile, drain pineapple, reserving 1/4 cup juice. In a large bowl, combine the pineapple, snow peas, carrot, cucumber and the reserved pineapple juice.

Drain the pasta; rinse with cold water. Add to pineapple mixture. Sprinkle with cilantro. Drizzle with salad dressing and toss to coat. Chill until serving. **Yield:** 5 servings.

This bright salad features sweet pineapple, crunchy vegetables and fresh cilantro in a tangy dressing with pasta. It requires just 15 minutes of prep, so it's perfect for a quick lunch or on-the-go dinner. —Mary Tallman Arbor Vitae, Wisconsin

30 Swiss Mushroom Orzo

prep/total time: 30 min.

1 cup uncooked orzo pasta
1 cup (4 ounces) shredded Swiss cheese
4 tablespoons cold butter, *divided*
2 teaspoons minced garlic
1/4 teaspoon salt
1/4 teaspoon pepper
1/2 cup sliced fresh mushrooms

Cook the orzo according to package directions. Meanwhile, in a food processor, combine the cheese, 3 tablespoons butter, garlic, salt and pepper; cover and process until smooth.

In a large saucepan, saute the mushrooms in remaining butter until tender. Drain orzo and add to mushrooms. Stir in cheese mixture until melted. **Yield:** 3 servings.

I often turn to this go-with-everything side dish as a substitute for rice or potatoes. It's also wonderful with roasted red peppers or steamed broccoli tossed in.
—Holly Bonds
Smyrna, Georgia

Cleaning Mushrooms: (tip)
Gently remove dirt by rubbing with a mushroom brush, or wipe mushrooms with a damp paper towel.

Apricot Spinach Salad

prep/total time: 10 min.

- 1 package (10 ounces) fresh baby spinach
- 1 cup canned apricot halves, drained and sliced
- 1/2 cup golden raisins
- 1/2 cup raspberry vinaigrette
- 1 teaspoon grated lemon peel

In a large salad bowl, combine the spinach, apricots and raisins. Drizzle with vinaigrette and sprinkle with lemon peel; toss to coat. **Yield:** 8 servings.

This yummy spinach salad is tossed with store-bought raspberry vinaigrette. Canned apricots and golden raisins add sweetness and color.
—Taste of Home Test Kitchen

Balsamic Asparagus

prep/total time: 15 min.

- 1 cup water
- 1 pound fresh asparagus, trimmed
- 2 tablespoons balsamic vinegar
- 1 tablespoon butter, melted
- 1 teaspoon minced garlic
- 1/4 teaspoon salt
- 1/4 teaspoon pepper

In a large skillet, bring water to a boil. Add asparagus; cover and cook for 2-4 minutes or until crisp-tender. In a small bowl, combine the vinegar, butter, garlic, salt and pepper. Drain asparagus; drizzle with balsamic mixture. **Yield:** 4 servings.

Pretty green spears of crisp-tender asparagus are drizzled with a balsamic vinegar mixture for a sensational side dish that's ready in no time.
—Taste of Home Test Kitchen

20 Warm Scallop Salad

prep/total time: 20 min.

- 1 pound sea scallops
- 1 tablespoon canola oil
- 1 medium sweet red pepper, julienned
- 2 teaspoons minced garlic
- 1/3 cup Italian salad dressing
- 1 tablespoon water
- 6 cups torn mixed salad greens
- 1/2 teaspoon pepper

In a large skillet, saute scallops in oil for 2 minutes on each side or until firm and opaque. Remove and keep warm. In the same skillet, saute red pepper and garlic for 2-3 minutes. Add salad dressing and water; cook 2-3 minutes longer, stirring occasionally.

Return scallops to the pan; cook for 2-3 minutes or until heated through. Place the greens in a salad bowl. Add scallop mixture and toss lightly; sprinkle with pepper. **Yield:** 4 servings.

Bottled dressing adds to the snappy preparation of this warm and wonderful salad that's healthy, too. I received the recipe from a friend years ago, and it always brings compliments when I serve it.
—Gertrudis Miller, Evansville, Indiana

(10) Simple Side Salad

prep/total time: 5 min.

2 cups torn leaf lettuce
1 medium tomato, chopped
1/2 cup chopped celery
Salad dressing of your choice

Divide the lettuce, tomato and celery among four salad plates. Drizzle with dressing. Serve immediately. **Yield:** 4 servings.

For a fast finishing touch to this speedy salad, top it with chopped tomato and your favorite salad dressing.
—Taste of Home
Test Kitchen

Don't Overdress Salads: (tip) Toss greens with salad dressing in a large bowl and serve immediately, or place greens in a salad bowl and pass the dressing at the table. Adding too much dressing will make a salad soggy and limp.

Microwave Potato Salad

prep: 20 min. + chilling

- 7 cups cubed red potatoes (about 2 pounds)
- 1 cup water
- 1-1/2 cups (6 ounces) shredded sharp cheddar cheese
- 1 cup mayonnaise
- 4 hard-cooked eggs, chopped
- 3/4 cup pimiento-stuffed olives, halved
- 3/4 cup chopped roasted sweet red peppers
- 1/2 cup sliced green onions
- 1/2 teaspoon pepper

Place potatoes in a shallow 2-qt. microwave-safe dish; add water. Cover and microwave on high for 9-11 minutes or until tender, stirring once. Drain and rinse in cold water.

In a large bowl, combine the remaining ingredients. Add potatoes and gently toss to coat. Cover and refrigerate for at least 1 hour before serving. **Yield:** 10 servings.

Editor's Note: This recipe was tested in a 1,100-watt microwave.

Microwaving potatoes for this tasty salad is a handy time-saver, especially in warm weather. I found the original recipe in an old cookbook and added roasted peppers and olives for color and zip. Chop your ingredients while the potatoes cook, and it's ready to chill in 20 minutes!
—Bonnie Carelli
Charlton Heights,
West Virginia

⏱20 Asparagus with Lemon Sauce

prep/total time: 15 min.

3 cups cut fresh asparagus (2-inch pieces)
1 can (8 ounces) sliced water chestnuts, drained
1/4 cup cream cheese, softened
2 tablespoons water
2 tablespoons milk
1/2 teaspoon grated lemon peel
1 tablespoon sliced almonds, toasted

Place asparagus and water chestnuts in a shallow microwave-safe dish; add 1/2 in. of water. Cover and microwave on high for 6-8 minutes or until asparagus is crisp-tender; drain and keep warm.

In a small microwave-safe bowl, combine the cream cheese, water, milk and lemon peel. Cover and microwave on high for 1 to 1-1/2 minutes or until heated through, stirring occasionally. Pour over asparagus mixture; sprinkle with almonds. **Yield:** 4 servings.

Editor's Note: This recipe was tested in a 1,100-watt microwave.

We didn't have an oven or stove in our first years of marriage, so we relied heavily on our microwave. This side dish of asparagus in a creamy lemon sauce was always a favorite.
—Janice Gerbitz
Woodland, California

Creamy Fruit Salad 20

prep/total time: 20 min.

2 medium apples, cut into 1-inch pieces
2 cups chopped peeled mango
2 cups halved seedless red grapes
3 tablespoons sour cream
3 tablespoons chopped walnuts, toasted

In a large bowl, combine apples, mango, grapes and sour cream. Refrigerate until serving. Just before serving, stir in the walnuts. **Yield:** 8 servings.

I'm on a low-fat diet. So I created this light, refreshing salad using my favorite fruits to take to church quiltings for lunch. Everyone loves it!
—Gerldean Cade
Brookhaven, Mississippi

(tip) **Picking Mangoes:** Mangoes are available most of the year. Select plump fruit with a sweet, fruity aroma. The skin of a ripe mango is green to yellow in color with a tinge of red.

30 Sweet Pasta Salad

prep/total time: 25 min.

3 cups uncooked penne pasta
1/2 cup heavy whipping cream
2 tablespoons confectioners' sugar
1/2 teaspoon vanilla extract
2 cups sliced fresh strawberries, *divided*
1 teaspoon canola oil
1/3 cup flaked coconut, toasted
4 cups torn salad greens
1/2 cup chopped walnuts, toasted

Cook pasta according to the package directions. Meanwhile, for dressing, combine the cream, confectioners' sugar, vanilla and 1/2 cup strawberries in a blender or food processor; cover and process until smooth and slightly thickened, about 30 seconds.

Drain the pasta; rinse in cold water. Place in a large bowl; add oil and toss to coat. Add coconut and remaining strawberries; toss gently. Place the greens in a serving bowl; top with pasta mixture. Drizzle with dressing; sprinkle with walnuts. **Yield:** 6-8 servings.

I first tasted this delightful salad several years ago at a pool party and begged the hostess for the recipe. Since then, I've served it many times and have always received rave reviews.
—Joan Hallford
North Richland Hills, Texas

Tossed Chicken Salad 🔟

prep/total time: 10 min.

1 package (10 ounces) hearts of
romaine salad mix
1 package (6 ounces) fresh baby
spinach
4 green onions, thinly sliced
8 slices ready-to-serve fully cooked
bacon strips, warmed and
crumbled
2 cans (15 ounces *each*) mandarin
oranges
1 package (9 ounces) frozen diced
cooked chicken, thawed

1 cup (4 ounces) shredded
part-skim mozzarella cheese
1/2 to 1 cup slivered almonds
2/3 cup ranch salad dressing
1/4 cup shredded Parmesan cheese,
optional

In a large salad bowl, combine the romaine,
spinach and onions. Add the bacon, oranges,
chicken, mozzarella cheese and almonds; toss
gently. Drizzle with dressing; sprinkle with
Parmesan cheese if desired. **Yield:** 8 servings.

*My husband is picky
about salads, but he loves
this combination of fruit,
meat and cheese. With
packaged greens and fully
cooked bacon, it goes
together quickly.*
—Vanetta Servoss
Southaven, Mississippi

(tip) **Try Other
Dressings:**
Change flavors
to suit your tastes
by trying a different
dressing like Italian,
raspberry vinaigrette or
honey mustard.

(30) Salsa Pasta 'n' Beans

prep/total time: 25 min.

8 ounces uncooked bow tie pasta
1/2 cup chopped onion
1 medium sweet yellow pepper, chopped
1 tablespoon olive oil
2 teaspoons minced garlic
1 can (16 ounces) red beans, rinsed and drained
3/4 cup vegetable broth
3/4 cup salsa
2 teaspoons ground cumin
1/3 cup minced fresh cilantro

Cook pasta according to package directions. Meanwhile, in a large skillet, saute onion and yellow pepper in oil for 3-4 minutes or until crisp-tender. Add garlic; cook 1-2 minutes longer or until tender.

Stir in the beans, broth, salsa and cumin. Bring to a boil. Reduce heat; simmer, uncovered, for 5-6 minutes or until heated through. Drain pasta; stir into bean mixture. Sprinkle with cilantro. **Yield:** 4 servings.

This warm side dish is well seasoned with cumin, cilantro and salsa, so it adds a little zip to dinnertime.
—Laura Perry
Exton, Pennsylvania

- - - - - - - - - - - - - - - - -

Spice It Up: For people who like even more spice, it's easy to change the salsa to a medium or hot variety. Or you can try using a can of black beans with jalapeno slices in place of the red beans.

(tip)

Festive Rice Medley 20

prep/total time: 15 min.

1-1/2 cups uncooked instant rice
1/4 cup chopped sweet red pepper
1/4 cup chopped sweet yellow pepper
2 teaspoons canola oil
2 tablespoons minced fresh cilantro
2 tablespoons chopped green onion
1/2 teaspoon minced garlic
1/4 teaspoon salt
1/4 teaspoon paprika, optional

Cook rice according to package directions. In a large skillet, saute the peppers in oil for 2-3 minutes or until tender. Add the cilantro, onion, garlic and salt. Stir in the rice and paprika if desired. Cook for 2-3 minutes or until heated through. **Yield:** 5 servings.

I punch up the flavor and nutrition of this versatile rice side dish with fresh cilantro and brightly colored peppers.
—Vicki Zobal
Georgetown, Texas

30 Cheddar-Almond Lettuce Salad

prep/total time: 30 min.

1/2 cup slivered almonds
3 tablespoons sugar
9 cups torn romaine
2 hard-cooked eggs, sliced
1 cup (4 ounces) shredded cheddar
    cheese

HONEY-MUSTARD DRESSING:

1/4 cup sugar
2 tablespoons white vinegar
2 tablespoons honey
1 tablespoon lemon juice
1/2 teaspoon onion powder
1/2 teaspoon celery seed
1/2 teaspoon ground mustard
1/2 teaspoon paprika
1/4 teaspoon salt
1/2 cup vegetable oil

In a small heavy skillet, combine almonds and sugar. Cook and stir over medium heat for 5-6 minutes or until nuts are coated and golden. Spread onto foil to cool. Divide romaine among salad plates; top with eggs and cheese.

In a blender, combine the sugar, vinegar, honey, lemon juice, onion powder, celery seed, mustard, paprika and salt. While processing, gradually add oil in a steady stream. Drizzle over salads; sprinkle with almonds. Serve immediately. **Yield:** 9 servings.

Sugared almonds and a homemade honey-mustard dressing make this salad a real standout. In fact, I keep slivered almonds in my freezer so I can whip it up on the spur of the moment. When I take it to picnics and potlucks, I get many requests for the recipe. For more nutrition and color, I sometimes add broccoli and tomatoes.
—Julia Musser
Lebanon, Pennsylvania

Fabulous Feta Salad ⏱30

prep/total time: 25 min.

2-1/2 cups uncooked bow tie pasta
4 cups torn romaine
1 cup cubed cooked chicken
1/2 cup crumbled feta cheese
1/2 cup Italian salad dressing

Cook pasta according to package directions; drain and rinse in cold water. In a large bowl, combine pasta, romaine, chicken and feta cheese. Drizzle with the dressing and toss to coat. **Yield:** 9 servings.

On busy days, I turn to this simple and pretty pasta salad when I need a fast, flavorful side dish. It's very good with Italian entrees.
—Amy Adams
Ogden, Utah

(tip) **About Feta:** A classic Greek cheese, feta has a tart, salty flavor. It's good with olives, vegetables, pasta salads, mixed green salads, seafood and chicken.

(30) Watermelon Tomato Salad

prep/total time: 25 min.

10 cups cubed seedless watermelon
2 pints yellow grape *or* pear tomatoes
1 medium red onion, chopped
1/2 cup minced fresh parsley
1/2 cup minced fresh basil
1/4 cup lime juice

In a large bowl, combine the watermelon, tomatoes and onion. In a small bowl, combine the parsley, basil and lime juice. Pour over the watermelon mixture and toss to coat. Refrigerate until serving. **Yield:** 16-18 servings.

Watermelon and tomatoes may seem an unlikely pairing, but they team up to make a winning combination in this eye-catching salad dressed with parsley, basil and lime juice. Slice up any leftover watermelon for juicy snacks.
—Matthew Denton
Seattle, Washington

- - - - - - - - - - - - - - -

Checking For Ripeness: (tip)
To test watermelon for ripeness, slap the side with the palm of your hand. A deep thump means it is ripe. One pound watermelon equals about 1 cup of cubes.

Buttery Brussels Sprouts

prep/total time: 15 min.

- 1 cup chicken broth
- 1/3 cup white wine *or* additional chicken broth
- 4-1/2 teaspoons butter
- 1/4 teaspoon white pepper, *divided*
- 2 packages (10 ounces *each*) frozen brussels sprouts
- 1/4 teaspoon salt

In a large saucepan, combine the broth, wine or additional broth, butter and 1/8 teaspoon white pepper; bring to a boil. Add brussels sprouts. Reduce heat; cover and simmer for 6-9 minutes or until tender. Drain and transfer to a bowl. Sprinkle with salt and remaining pepper. **Yield:** 6 servings.

I give a dressy touch to this simple stovetop side dish by adding a splash of white wine. —Polly Heer
Cabot, Arkansas

Sesame Green Beans

prep/total time: 15 min.

- 3/4 pound fresh green beans, trimmed
- 1/2 cup water
- 1 tablespoon butter
- 1 tablespoon soy sauce
- 2 teaspoons sesame seeds, toasted

In a large saucepan, bring beans and water to a boil; reduce heat to medium. Cover and cook for 5-7 minutes or until the beans are crisp-tender; drain. Add butter, soy sauce and sesame seeds; toss to coat. **Yield:** 6 servings.

For me, the most time-consuming part of preparing this side dish is picking the green beans in the garden. My family loves their fresh taste, and I love that they're fast to fix! —Jeanne Bennett
North Richland Hills, Texas

Catalina Parmesan Salad

prep/total time: 10 min.

- 2 cups torn leaf lettuce
- 2/3 cup chopped fresh tomato
- 1/4 cup shredded Parmesan cheese
- 1/4 cup Catalina salad dressing

Divide the lettuce and tomato among four small salad plates. Sprinkle with Parmesan cheese and drizzle with dressing. **Yield:** 4 servings.

Feel free to toss in any additional salad fixings you have on hand, such as croutons, sliced green pepper or chopped cucumber. —Taste of Home Test Kitchen

⑳ Garlic Oregano Zucchini

prep/total time: 15 min.

1 teaspoon minced garlic
2 tablespoons canola oil
4 medium zucchini, sliced
1 teaspoon dried oregano
1/2 teaspoon salt
1/8 teaspoon pepper

In a large skillet, cook and stir the garlic in oil over medium heat for 1 minute. Add the zucchini, oregano, salt and pepper. Cook and stir for 4-6 minutes or until the zucchini is crisp-tender. **Yield:** 4 servings.

This flavorful zucchini side dish complements almost any meal. You could use half yellow summer squash for a colorful variation.
—Teresa Kraus
Cortez, Colorado

Preparing Zucchini: Select firm, plump zucchini with bright green skin. Wash but do not peel. Remove the stem and blossom ends and cut into slices.

Pea 'n' Peanut Salad 20

prep/total time: 15 min.

1 package (10 ounces) frozen peas,
   thawed
1 cup dry roasted peanuts
1 cup chopped celery
6 bacon strips, cooked and
   crumbled
1/4 cup chopped red onion
1/2 cup mayonnaise
1/4 cup prepared zesty Italian salad
   dressing

In a large bowl, combine the peas, peanuts, celery, bacon and onion. In a small bowl, combine the mayonnaise and Italian dressing. Pour over salad and toss to coat. Chill until serving. **Yield:** 5 servings.

Even people who don't like peas—including my own children—love this crunchy combo. I love the fact that it's so easy and makes a refreshing alternative to more traditional salads. A friend gave me the recipe years ago, and I've been making it ever since.
—Laurinda Nelson
Phoenix, Arizona

⑳ Basil Walnut Fettuccine

prep/total time: 20 min.

- 6 ounces uncooked fettuccine
- 6 ounces uncooked spinach fettuccine
- 1 teaspoon minced garlic
- 6 tablespoons butter, *divided*
- 1/4 cup finely chopped walnuts, toasted
- 1 tablespoon minced fresh basil *or* 1 teaspoon dried basil
- 1/4 teaspoon salt
- 1/8 teaspoon pepper

Cook both kinds of fettuccine according to package directions. In a large skillet, saute the garlic in 1 tablespoon butter for 1 minute. Add the walnuts, basil, salt, pepper and remaining butter; cook and stir for 2 minutes. Drain the fettuccine; add to skillet and toss to coat. **Yield:** 6 servings.

This pasta side dish is studded with toasted nuts and lightly flavored with garlic and basil. The combination of regular and spinach fettuccine is eye-catching, but you can use any flavor or shape of pasta you have on hand.
—Taste of Home
Test Kitchen

Toasting Nuts: **(tip)**
Spread nuts in a 15-in. x 10-in. x 1-in. baking pan. Bake at 350° for 5-10 minutes or until lightly browned, stirring occasionally.

Italian Veggie Skillet 30

prep/total time: 25 min.

1 medium yellow summer squash,
  cut into 1/4-inch slices
1/2 cup sliced fresh mushrooms
1 tablespoon olive oil
1 cup cherry tomatoes, halved
1/2 teaspoon salt
1/2 teaspoon minced garlic
2 tablespoons minced fresh parsley
1-1/2 teaspoons minced fresh rosemary
  or 1/2 teaspoon dried rosemary,
  crushed
1-1/2 teaspoons minced fresh thyme
  or 1/2 teaspoon dried thyme
1-1/2 teaspoons plus 2 tablespoons
  minced fresh basil, *divided*

2 tablespoons sliced green onion
2 tablespoons grated Parmesan
  cheese

In a large skillet, saute squash and mushrooms in oil for 4-5 minutes or until tender. Add the tomatoes, salt and garlic. Reduce heat; simmer, uncovered, for 6-8 minutes.

Stir in the parsley, rosemary, thyme and 1-1/2 teaspoons basil; cook 1-2 minutes longer or until heated through. Transfer to a serving bowl. Sprinkle with onion and remaining basil; lightly toss. Sprinkle with Parmesan cheese. **Yield:** 2-3 servings.

Although I'm retired, I like recipes that are fast to prepare. This side dish is ready in no time and incorporates vegetables and herbs from our garden for a refreshing taste. —Josephine Piro Easton, Pennsylvania

Sweet-and-Sour Squash Salad

prep/total time: 20 min.

2 medium yellow summer squash, thinly sliced
2 medium zucchini, thinly sliced
1 cup chopped celery
1 cup chopped red onion
1/2 cup *each* chopped green and sweet red pepper

DRESSING:
3/4 cup sugar
1/2 cup cider vinegar
1/4 cup olive oil
2 tablespoons ranch salad dressing mix
1/4 to 1/2 teaspoon pepper
1/8 teaspoon salt

In a large salad bowl, combine the yellow squash, zucchini, celery, onion and peppers. In a jar with a tight-fitting lid, combine the dressing ingredients; shake well. Drizzle over the vegetables and toss to coat. Chill until serving. Serve with a slotted spoon. **Yield:** 7 servings.

This salad is a cherished family recipe. It's a good way to get kids to eat squash and goes over well with all ages. Let it sit overnight for the best flavor.
—Anita West
Levelland, Texas

Antipasto Picnic Salad

prep: 30 min. **cook:** 15 min.

1 package (16 ounces) medium pasta shells
2 jars (16 ounces *each*) giardiniera
1 pound fresh broccoli florets
1/2 pound part-skim mozzarella cheese, cubed
1/2 pound hard salami, cubed
1/2 pound deli ham, cubed
2 packages (3-1/2 ounces *each*) sliced pepperoni, halved
1 large green pepper, cut into chunks
1 can (6 ounces) pitted ripe olives, drained

DRESSING:
1/2 cup olive oil
1/4 cup red wine vinegar
2 tablespoons lemon juice
1 teaspoon Italian seasoning
1 teaspoon coarsely ground pepper
1/2 teaspoon salt

Cook the pasta according to package directions. Meanwhile, drain giardiniera, reserving 3/4 cup liquid. In a large bowl, combine giardiniera, broccoli, mozzarella, salami, ham, pepperoni, green pepper and olives.

Drain pasta and rinse in cold water; stir into meat mixture. For dressing, in a small bowl, whisk oil, vinegar, lemon juice, Italian seasoning, pepper, salt and reserved giardiniera liquid. Pour over salad and toss to coat. Chill until serving. **Yield:** 25 servings.

Everybody just loves this tempting blend of meats, vegetables and pasta. It goes together in no time, serves a crowd and tastes as delicious at room temperature as it does chilled. Also, it's chunky enough for the kids to pick out any individual ingredient they don't like.
—Michele Larson
Baden, Pennsylvania

(tip) **About Giardiniera:** Giardiniera, a pickled vegetable mixture, is available in mild and hot varieties and can be found in the Italian or pickle section of your grocery store.

⏱30 Layered Salad Reuben-Style

prep/total time: 30 min.

4-1/2 teaspoons butter, melted
1/8 teaspoon salt
1/8 teaspoon pepper
2 cups cubed rye bread
1 package (16 ounces) ready-to-serve salad greens
2 cups chopped pastrami
1 large tomato, diced
1/2 cup sauerkraut, rinsed and well drained
1/4 cup thinly sliced green onions
1 bottle (8 ounces) Thousand Island salad dressing
3/4 cup shredded Swiss cheese

In a bowl, combine the butter, salt and pepper. Add bread cubes and toss to coat. Arrange in a single layer in an ungreased 15-in. x 10-in. x 1-in. baking pan. Bake at 400° for 8-10 minutes or until golden brown, stirring occasionally. Cool.

In a large salad bowl, layer half of the salad greens, pastrami, tomato, sauerkraut, onions and dressing; repeat layers. Sprinkle with croutons and Swiss cheese. **Yield:** 12 servings.

Here's a fun twist on the traditional seven-layer salad that's great for large gatherings any time of year. It combines lettuce and tomato with Reuben sandwich fixings. I like to buy pastrami in 1/4-inch slices at the deli counter and chop it up at home, but you can use leftover corned beef instead.
—Amy Smith
Avon, Connecticut

Hash Brown Apple Pancake

prep/total time: 20 min.

- 1-1/4 cups frozen shredded hash brown potatoes, thawed
- 1/2 cup finely chopped apple
- 1/4 cup finely chopped onion
- 1 tablespoon minced chives
- 1/4 teaspoon salt
- 1/4 teaspoon pepper
- 2 tablespoons butter, *divided*
- 2 tablespoons vegetable oil, *divided*
- 1/2 cup shredded Swiss cheese

In a small bowl, combine the hash browns, apple, onion, chives, salt and pepper. In a large nonstick skillet, melt 1 tablespoon butter with 1 tablespoon oil over medium-high heat. Spread half of the hash brown mixture in an even layer in skillet. Sprinkle with cheese; top with remaining hash browns. Press mixture gently into skillet. Cook for 5 minutes or until bottom is browned.

Invert pancake onto a plate. Heat remaining butter and oil in the skillet. Slide pancake, browned side up, into skillet. Cook 5 minutes longer or until bottom is browned and cheese is melted. Slide pancake onto a plate; cut into wedges. **Yield:** 4 servings.

Wedges of this potato pancake will make a fast and fabulous side dish the whole family will savor. Laced with onion, chives and Swiss cheese, they take only minutes and would go well with all kinds of entrees.
—*Taste of Home Test Kitchen*

Strawberry Spinach Salad

prep/total time: 10 min.

- 1 package (10 ounces) fresh spinach, torn
- 2 cups sliced fresh strawberries
- 1 cup sliced fresh mushrooms
- 1/3 cup real bacon bits
- 1/3 cup raspberry vinaigrette

In a large salad bowl, combine the spinach, strawberries, mushrooms and bacon. Drizzle with vinaigrette and toss to coat. **Yield:** 6 servings.

Tossed with fresh strawberries, mushrooms and bacon bits, this spinach salad looks and tastes special enough for company. —*Taste of Home Test Kitchen*

⓴ Creamy Mushroom Bow Ties

prep/total time: 20 min.

6 cups uncooked bow tie pasta
1 pound sliced fresh mushrooms
1/2 teaspoon salt
1/4 teaspoon pepper
2 tablespoons butter
1 package (4.4 ounces) garlic-herb cheese spread
1/4 cup chicken broth

Cook pasta according to package directions. Meanwhile, in a large skillet, saute the mushrooms, salt and pepper in butter until tender. Add cheese spread and broth; cook and stir until blended. Drain pasta; add to skillet and toss to coat. **Yield:** 9 servings.

This pasta side dish has become one of our favorites. It is so easy, but it tastes like it took much longer in the kitchen than it does.
—Dodi Walker
Peachtree City, Georgia

Two-Cheese Baked Potatoes ⏱30

prep/total time: 25 min.

4 large baking potatoes
1/4 cup shredded Parmesan cheese
1/4 cup shredded part-skim
    mozzarella cheese
1/4 teaspoon salt
1/4 teaspoon pepper
4 teaspoons butter
1/2 teaspoon dried parsley flakes

Scrub and pierce potatoes; place on a microwave-safe plate. Microwave, uncovered, on high for 13-15 minutes or until tender, turning once. Meanwhile, combine the cheeses, salt and pepper in a small bowl.

Cut an X in the top of each potato; fluff pulp with a fork. Top with butter and cheese mixture; sprinkle with parsley. **Yield:** 4 servings.

Editor's Note: This recipe was tested in a 1,100-watt microwave.

Here's an easy way to top tender baked potatoes that are cooked in the microwave in minutes.
—Taste of Home
Test Kitchen

(tip) **Best Potatoes for Baking:** Russets and Idahos are good baking potatoes. They have a high starch content that produces a fluffy, dry texture when baked.

 🕙 Broccoli Cranberry Slaw

prep/total time: 10 min.

1 package (12 ounces) broccoli coleslaw mix
1 package (3 ounces) dried cranberries
6 green onions, cut into 1/2-inch pieces
1/4 cup coleslaw salad dressing

In a large bowl, combine the coleslaw mix, cranberries and onions. Add dressing and toss to coat. Refrigerate until serving. **Yield:** 8 servings.

I need just four items to toss together this crunchy coleslaw that gets a sweet twist from dried cranberries. It's lightly coated with convenient prepared dressing.
—Marie Siciliano
Westerly, Rhode Island

Turkey Wild Rice Salad 30

prep/total time: 25 min.

2 cups cubed cooked turkey breast
2 cups cooked wild rice
1 cup seedless red grapes, halved
1/2 cup diced sweet red pepper
1/2 cup chopped celery
1/2 cup dried cherries
1/2 cup coarsely chopped pecans, toasted
4 green onions, sliced
1/3 cup raspberry vinaigrette

In a large bowl, combine the first eight ingredients. Drizzle with the vinaigrette and toss to coat. Refrigerate until serving. **Yield:** 7 servings.

Serve up a medley of textures and tastes with this colorful luncheon idea. Crunchy celery, red pepper and pecans combine with juicy grapes, dried cherries, wild rice and leftover turkey in this standout salad. —Taste of Home Test Kitchen

----

(tip) **Rice Replacement:** If you don't have wild rice on hand, brown rice is an easy substitution.

⏱30 Artichoke Steak Salad

prep/total time: 25 min.

2 pounds boneless beef sirloin steaks
12 cherry tomatoes
1 medium red onion, sliced
1 jar (7-1/2 ounces) marinated artichoke hearts, drained and sliced
1 cup sliced fresh mushrooms
1/4 cup red wine vinegar
1/4 cup olive oil
1 teaspoon sugar
1 teaspoon salt
1/2 teaspoon dried oregano
1/2 teaspoon dried rosemary, crushed
1/2 teaspoon pepper
1/2 teaspoon minced garlic
6 cups torn fresh spinach

Grill steaks, covered, over medium heat or broil 4 in. from the heat for 5-7 minutes on each side or until meat reaches desired doneness (for medium-rare, a meat thermometer should read 145°; medium, 160°; well-done, 170°).

Meanwhile, in a large bowl, combine the tomatoes, onion, artichokes and mushrooms. In a small bowl, whisk the vinegar, oil, sugar, salt, oregano, rosemary, pepper and garlic. Pour over vegetable mixture and toss to coat.

Thinly slice steaks across the grain. Add beef and spinach to vegetable mixture; toss to coat. **Yield:** 6 servings.

Using your outdoor grill to cook the sirloin steaks for this satisfying main-dish salad is sure to help keep your kitchen cool. We tossed the sliced beef with marinated artichoke hearts, fresh spinach, cherry tomatoes, mushrooms and a nicely seasoned homemade vinaigrette.
—Taste of Home Test Kitchen

Broccoli Saute 20

prep/total time: 15 min.

1/2 cup chopped onion
1/2 cup julienned sweet red pepper
2 tablespoons olive oil
6 cups fresh broccoli florets
2/3 cup water
1-1/2 teaspoons minced garlic
1/4 teaspoon salt
1/4 teaspoon pepper

In a large skillet, saute onion and red pepper in oil for 2-3 minutes or until crisp-tender. Stir in the broccoli, water, garlic, salt and pepper. Cover and cook over medium heat for 5-6 minutes or until broccoli is crisp-tender. **Yield:** 5 servings.

I invented this recipe while looking for a different treatment for broccoli that was lower in sodium. Quick and tasty, it's a colorful accompaniment to any dinner.
—Jim MacNeal
Waterloo, New York

Don't Overcook Broccoli: Overcooking broccoli will cause it to break apart, lose its color, diminish its taste and will cause the loss of many nutrients.

⏱30 Lemon-Linguine Shrimp Salad

prep/total time: 30 min.

1/4 cup olive oil
2 tablespoons white wine vinegar
2 tablespoons minced fresh parsley
1/2 to 1 teaspoon cayenne pepper
1/2 teaspoon dried oregano
1/4 teaspoon salt
1 pound cooked small shrimp, peeled and deveined
1 package (16 ounces) linguine
1/2 pound fresh asparagus, trimmed and cut into 1-inch pieces

LEMON DRESSING:
2/3 cup olive oil
2/3 cup shredded Parmesan cheese
1/2 cup lemon juice

1 tablespoon grated lemon peel
1/3 cup minced fresh basil

In a large resealable plastic bag, combine the oil, vinegar, parsley, cayenne, oregano and salt; add shrimp. Seal bag and turn to coat; set aside.

Cook linguine according to the package directions, adding asparagus during the last 3 minutes; drain and rinse in cold water. In a large bowl, combine the oil, Parmesan cheese, lemon juice and lemon peel; add linguine mixture and toss to coat.

Drain and discard marinade; add shrimp to linguine. Cover and refrigerate until serving. Sprinkle with basil. **Yield:** 6 servings.

This summery medley of spicy shrimp, fresh asparagus and pasta is subtly splashed with lemon. It adds a touch of elegance to any outdoor gathering or luncheon. If you make it ahead, add the basil just before serving.
—*Laureen Pittman
Riverside, California*

Roasted Italian Vegetables

prep/total time: 25 min.

1 **medium zucchini, cut into 1/4-inch slices**
1-1/2 **cups sliced baby portobello mushrooms**
1 **medium sweet orange pepper, julienned**
1 **tablespoon olive oil**
1 **tablespoon butter, melted**
1 **teaspoon Italian seasoning**
1/2 **teaspoon salt**
1/8 **teaspoon pepper**

In a large bowl, combine the zucchini, mushrooms and orange pepper. Add the remaining ingredients and toss to coat.

Arrange vegetables in a single layer in a 15-in. x 10-in. x 1-in. baking pan coated with nonstick cooking spray. Bake, uncovered, at 450° for 15-20 minutes or until tender, stirring occasionally. **Yield:** 4 servings.

This medley of oven-baked vegetables is ideal with fish or most any meat. —*Taste of Home Test Kitchen*

(tip) **Vary the Veggies:** Zucchini and orange pepper make this side dish colorful, but feel free to substitute yellow summer squash or red or green pepper.

Tuscan Bean Salad

prep/total time: 30 min.

2 **cans (15 ounces *each*) white kidney *or* cannellini beans, rinsed and drained**
1 **jar (6-1/2 ounces) marinated artichoke hearts, undrained**
1 **cup roasted sweet red peppers, cut into 1-inch strips**
3/4 **cup sliced ripe olives**
1/2 **cup chopped red onion**
1/4 **cup oil-packed sun-dried tomatoes, chopped**
2 **tablespoons olive oil**
2 **tablespoons white balsamic vinegar**
1/4 **teaspoon salt**
1/4 **teaspoon pepper**
1/4 **cup fresh basil leaves, thinly sliced**

In a salad bowl, combine the first 10 ingredients. Refrigerate for 20 minutes or until serving. Stir in basil. Serve with a slotted spoon. **Yield:** 6 servings.

My sister-in-law gave me this delicious recipe. It's a can't-miss salad that's jam-packed with wonderful flavor and the easy convenience of canned and jarred ingredients. —*Cori Rothe, Livermore, California*

⑩ Tossed Salad with Pine Nuts

prep/total time: 10 min.

5 cups spring mix salad greens
1 small red onion, thinly sliced
1 cup (4 ounces) crumbled blue cheese
1/2 cup pine nuts, toasted
1/4 to 1/3 cup raspberry vinaigrette

In a large salad bowl, combine the greens and onion. Sprinkle with the blue cheese and pine nuts. Drizzle with the vinaigrette; toss to coat. Serve immediately. **Yield:** 6-7 servings.

This salad has lots of blue cheese flavor and a crunch from pine nuts. Topped with raspberry vinaigrette, it couldn't be much easier to toss together on a busy night.
—Alice Tremont
Rochester Hills, Michigan

- - - - - - - - - - - - - - - - -

Serving Suggestions: (tip) Serve this salad on special occasions, and it will always get compliments. Adding grilled chicken turns it into a fuss-free main dish.

desserts

Coconut Ice Cream Torte, pg. 218

Raspberry Lime Slush

prep: 15 min. + freezing

3/4 cup sugar
2 cups water, *divided*
1 cup fresh *or* frozen raspberries, thawed
1/2 cup lime juice
3 cups ginger ale, chilled

In a small saucepan, combine sugar and 1/2 cup water. Cook and stir over high heat until sugar is completely dissolved. Remove from the heat. Press raspberries through a sieve; discard seeds.

In a large bowl, combine the raspberry puree, sugar syrup, lime juice and remaining water. Transfer to a 1-qt. freezer container. Cover and freeze for 12 hours, stirring occasionally. May be frozen for up to 3 months.

To serve, combine the raspberry mixture and ginger ale in a 2-qt. pitcher. Or for one serving, combine 1/2 cup raspberry mixture and 1/2 cup ginger ale in a glass. **Yield:** 6 servings.

For a cool ending to a meal, scoop this bright pink slush into stemmed glasses, then drizzle with ginger ale. The lime adds a little zing for a sweet-tart taste that's especially refreshing.
—*Taste of Home Test Kitchen*

Very Berry Pie

prep: 15 min. + chilling

1-3/4 cups reduced-fat whipped
    topping, *divided*
  1 reduced-fat graham cracker crust
    (8 inches)
  1 cup fresh raspberries
  1 cup fresh blueberries
Sugar substitute equivalent to 1
    tablespoon sugar
  1 cup cold fat-free milk
  1 package (1 ounce) sugar-free
    instant white chocolate pudding
    mix

Spread 1/4 cup whipped topping into the crust. Combine berries and sugar substitute; spoon 1 cup over topping. In a bowl, whisk the milk and pudding mix for 2 minutes; let stand for 2 minutes or until soft-set. Spoon over berries. Spread with remaining whipped topping. Top with remaining berries. Refrigerate for 45 minutes or until set. **Yield:** 8 servings.

Editor's Note: This recipe was tested with Splenda No Calorie Sweetener.

I came up with this quick pie when I needed a low-fat dessert for a get-together. My husband picked this pie over apple pie, which he generally prefers. He raves about how good it is.
—Becky Thompson
Maryville, Tennessee

(tip) **Take Care With Berries:** Berries are fragile and very perishable. Before refrigerating, sort through and discard any crushed, mushy or moldy fruit.

Salty Peanut Squares

prep: 15 min. + cooling

- 1 package (10 ounces) corn chips, slightly crushed, *divided*
- 1 cup unsalted peanuts, *divided*
- 1 cup light corn syrup
- 1 cup sugar
- 1 cup peanut butter
- 1/2 cup milk chocolate chips, melted

Place half of the corn chips and peanuts in a greased 13-in. x 9-in. x 2-in. pan; set aside. In a saucepan, bring the corn syrup and sugar to a boil. Stir in peanut butter until blended. Drizzle half over corn chip mixture in pan.

Add remaining corn chips and peanuts to remaining syrup; stir until combined. Spoon over mixture in pan; press down lightly. Drizzle with melted chocolate. Cool before cutting. **Yield:** 2 dozen.

If your family likes corn chips, they'll love the sweet and salty blend in these fast-to-fix bars. They make great take-along treats for picnics or tailgate parties and are so easy, the kids may want to make their own batch.
—Wanda Borgen
Minot, North Dakota

Cinnamon Apple Tart

prep: 15 min. **bake:** 20 min. + cooling

- 1 large apple, peeled and chopped
- 1 teaspoon lemon juice
- 1 sheet refrigerated pie pastry
- 2 tablespoons apple jelly
- 2 tablespoons sugar
- 1/4 cup cinnamon baking chips
- 1/3 cup sliced almonds
- 1 teaspoon milk

ICING:

- 1 cup confectioners' sugar
- 1/4 teaspoon almond extract
- 1 to 2 tablespoons milk

In a small bowl, toss apple with lemon juice; set aside. On a lightly floured surface, roll pastry into a 14-in. circle. Transfer to a parchment paper-lined baking sheet. Spread jelly to within 2 in. of edges. Sprinkle with apple mixture, sugar, baking chips and almonds. Fold up edges of pastry over filling, leaving center uncovered. Brush folded pastry with milk.

Bake at 400° for 20-25 minutes or until golden brown. Use parchment paper to slide tart onto a wire rack to cool. In a small bowl, combine confectioners' sugar, extract and enough milk to achieve desired consistency. Drizzle over tart. **Yield:** 6 servings.

I got the idea for this delicious dessert from a lovely Italian woman who's also a fabulous cook. It's so simple to make. —Stacie Blemings Califon, New Jersey

(tip) **Another Tasty Topper:** An easy variation is to use strawberry jam and walnuts, then skip the icing.

Candy Cookie Cups

prep: 15 min. **bake:** 15 min. + cooling

1/2 cup finely chopped macadamia
    nuts
1 package (18 ounces) individually
    portioned refrigerated white chip
    macadamia nut cookie dough
24 miniature peanut butter cups

Sprinkle macadamia nuts into 24 greased miniature muffin cups, 1 teaspoon in each. Cut each portion of cookie dough in half; place each half in a muffin cup.

Bake at 325° for 11-13 minutes or until golden brown. Immediately place a peanut butter cup in each cookie; press down gently. Cool completely before removing from pans to wire racks. **Yield:** 2 dozen.

These rich bites take advantage of time-saving convenience products for speedy prep.
—*Sarah Vasques*
Milford, New Hampshire

Peaches 'n' Cream Pizza

prep: 15 min. **bake:** 30 min. + cooling

- 1 tube (8 ounces) refrigerated crescent roll dough
- 1 package (8 ounces) cream cheese, softened
- 1/2 cup sugar
- 1/2 teaspoon almond extract
- 1 can (21 ounces) peach pie filling
- 1/2 cup all-purpose flour
- 1/4 cup packed brown sugar
- 3 tablespoons cold butter
- 1/2 cup sliced almonds

Separate crescent dough into eight triangles. Press onto a greased 12-in. pizza pan; seal seams. Bake at 375° for 8-10 minutes or until edges are golden. Cool slightly on a wire rack.

In a small mixing bowl, beat the cream cheese, sugar and extract until smooth. Spread over crust. Top with pie filling. In a small bowl, combine flour and brown sugar; cut in butter until crumbly. Sprinkle over peaches. Top with almonds. Bake for 20-25 minutes or until golden brown. Cool. Refrigerate leftovers. **Yield:** 12-16 servings.

With a crispy crust, this sweet pizza is topped with almond-flavored cream cheese and peach pie filling. I get rave reviews every time I serve it. —Linda Patrick Houston, Texas

- -

Pretty Garnishes:
Try garnishing wedges of this dessert pizza with whipped cream, extra almonds or other nuts, fresh peach slices or sprigs of mint.

Fried Ice Cream

prep: 30 min. + freezing

- 1 sheet refrigerated pie pastry
- 1-1/2 teaspoons sugar
- 1 teaspoon ground cinnamon
- 1 quart vanilla **ice cream**
- Oil for deep-fat frying
- 1/2 cup honey

Unroll pastry onto an ungreased 15-in. x 10-in. x 1-in. baking pan. Combine sugar and cinnamon; sprinkle over pastry. Prick thoroughly with a fork. Bake at 400° for 10-12 minutes or until lightly browned. Cool on a wire rack for 5 minutes.

Place pastry in a large resealable plastic bag; coarsely crush. Transfer to a shallow bowl. Using a 1/2-cup ice cream scoop, form eight scoops of ice cream. Roll in pastry crumbs. Cover and freeze for 2 hours or until firm.

In an electric skillet or deep-fat fryer, heat oil to 375°. Fry ice cream balls for 8-10 seconds or until golden. Drain on paper towels. Immediately place in chilled bowls; drizzle with honey and serve. **Yield:** 8 servings.

Refrigerated pie crust sprinkled with cinnamon-sugar, baked and crumbled, makes short work of this fun dessert. —Taste of Home Test Kitchen

Cookie Fruit Baskets

prep: 15 min. **bake:** 10 min. per batch + cooling

1/4 cup butter
1/4 cup packed brown sugar
1/4 cup light corn syrup
3-1/2 tablespoons all-purpose flour
1/2 cup ground pecans
1/2 teaspoon vanilla extract
Vanilla ice cream and fresh raspberries
    and blueberries

In a small saucepan, melt butter over low heat. Stir in brown sugar and corn syrup; cook and stir until mixture comes to a boil. Remove from the heat. Stir in flour. Fold in pecans and vanilla. Drop by tablespoonfuls 3 in. apart onto parchment paper-lined baking sheets.

Bake at 325° for 8-10 minutes or until golden brown. Cool for 30-60 seconds; peel cookies off paper. Immediately drape over inverted 6-oz. custard cups; cool completely. Scoop ice cream into baskets; top with raspberries and blueberries. **Yield:** 12 servings.

When visiting a friend, I helped organize her recipe collection into scrapbooks. When I found this recipe, I asked to copy it, then served the elegant dessert at my bridge club luncheon to oohs and aahs.   —Theresa Myslicki
North Fort Myers, Florida

Chocolate Cranberry Cheesecake

prep: 15 min. **bake:** 30 min. + chilling

1-1/3 cups chocolate wafer crumbs
1/4 cup sugar
1/4 cup butter, melted
FILLING:
2 packages (8 ounces *each*) cream cheese, softened
1/2 cup sugar
3/4 cup sour cream
1 tablespoon cornstarch
2 eggs, lightly beaten
1 cup whole-berry cranberry sauce
1/4 cup hot fudge ice cream topping, warmed

In a small bowl, combine wafer crumbs, sugar and butter. Press onto the bottom and 1 in. up the sides of a greased 9-in. springform pan; set aside.

In a large mixing bowl, beat cream cheese and sugar until smooth. Add sour cream and cornstarch; beat well. Add eggs; beat on low speed just until combined. Fold in cranberry sauce. Pour into crust. Place pan on a baking sheet.

Bake at 325° for 30-35 minutes or until center is almost set. Cool on a wire rack for 10 minutes. Carefully run a knife around edge of pan to loosen; cool 1 hour longer. Refrigerate overnight. Remove sides of pan. Pipe dessert plates with fudge topping; top with cheesecake. Refrigerate leftovers. **Yield:** 10-12 servings.

I think the ultimate dessert any time of the year is cheesecake. I worked at a specialty bakery that offered 23 different cheesecakes, but not a chocolate-cranberry flavor like this one.
—Darlene Brenden
Salem, Oregon

(tip) **Doneness Test:** A cheesecake is done when the edges are slightly puffed and when the center (about 1 in. diameter) jiggles slightly when the side of the pan is tapped with a spoon. The retained heat will continue to cook the center while the cheesecake is cooling.

20 Banana Chocolate Parfaits

prep/total time: 20 min.

3 medium bananas, sliced
1/4 cup lemon juice
2 cups cold fat-free milk
1 package (1.4 ounces) sugar-free instant chocolate pudding mix
1 cup (8 ounces) reduced-fat sour cream
1-1/2 cups reduced-fat whipped topping
8 chocolate wafers, crushed

In a small bowl, combine bananas and lemon juice; let stand for 5 minutes. In another bowl, whisk the milk and pudding mix for 2 minutes. Refrigerate for 5 minutes. Stir in sour cream.

Drain bananas. Place half of the banana slices in eight parfait glasses; layer with pudding mixture, whipped topping, chocolate wafer crumbs and remaining banana slices. Refrigerate until serving. **Yield:** 8 servings.

Chocolate and banana pair deliciously in this creamy combination. With chocolate pudding and a crunchy cookie topping, these pretty parfaits are sure to satisfy any sweet-tooth craving.
—Taste of Home Test Kitchen

- - - - - - - - - - - - - -

Sweet Substitution: **(tip)** You can also prepare these parfaits with vanilla pudding and vanilla wafers in place of the chocolate.

Almond Coconut Bars

prep: 15 min. bake: 20 min. + chilling

1-1/2 cups graham cracker crumbs
1/2 cup butter, melted
1 can (14 ounces) sweetened condensed milk
1 package (7 ounces) flaked coconut
2 cups (12 ounces) semisweet chocolate chips
1/2 cup peanut butter
24 whole almonds

In a small bowl, combine the graham cracker crumbs and butter. Press into an ungreased 13-in. x 9-in. x 2-in. baking pan. Combine milk and coconut; carefully spread over crust. Bake at 350° for 18-20 minutes or until lightly browned.

In a microwave-safe bowl, combine the chocolate chips and peanut butter. Microwave on high for 1 minute; stir. Microwave 30-60 seconds longer or until chips are melted; stir until smooth. Spread over warm bars. Garnish with almonds. Refrigerate for 1 hour before cutting. **Yield:** 2 dozen.

This is good to take to a picnic or potluck supper. I think they taste like Almond Joy candy bars. If you omit the almonds, they'll taste like Mounds bars. —Dolores Skrout Summerhill, Pennsylvania

Lemon Strawberry Tarts

prep: 5 min. **bake:** 15 min. + cooling

1 package (18 ounces) refrigerated sugar cookie dough
3/4 cup chilled lemon curd
6 large fresh strawberries, sliced
Whipped cream

Cut the cookie dough into 1/2-in. slices. Place 2 in. apart on ungreased baking sheets. Bake at 350° for 11-12 minutes or until lightly browned. Remove to wire racks to cool.

Spread six cookies with 2 tablespoons lemon curd. Garnish with strawberries and whipped cream. Save remaining cookies for another use. **Yield:** 6 tarts.

These pretty tarts only look like they took some time to prepare! They're even nice enough to serve to guests.
—Taste of Home Test Kitchen

- - - - - - - - - - - - - - - - -

Cookie Clues: You'll have leftover cookies after baking the refrigerated cookie dough. Either put them in the cookie jar for a quick snack, or freeze them and make this dessert again the following week. For an even easier treat, purchase cookies from the bakery instead of making them yourself.

(tip)

Deep-Fried Cherry Pies 30

prep/total time: 30 min.

1 cup all-purpose flour
1/4 teaspoon baking powder
1/4 teaspoon salt
2 tablespoons shortening
1/3 cup boiling water
1 cup cherry pie filling
Oil for deep-fat frying
1/4 cup maple syrup
1/4 cup whipped topping

In a small bowl, combine the flour, baking powder and salt. Cut in shortening until mixture resembles coarse crumbs. Stir in water just until moistened. Turn onto a lightly floured surface; knead 8-10 times.

Divide dough into four portions; roll each into an 8-in. circle. Place 1/4 cup of pie filling in the center of each circle. Fold dough over filling; secure with toothpicks.

In an electric skillet, heat 1 in. of oil to 375°. Fry pies, folded side down, in the oil for 2-3 minutes or until lightly browned. Turn and fry 2-3 minutes longer. Drain on paper towels. Remove the toothpicks. Serve with syrup and whipped topping. **Yield:** 4 servings.

With a flaky homemade crust, these stuffed cherry pies always make a quick dessert. My family loves them after dinner or as a snack, but they're also wonderful for my husband's take-along lunch. —Monica Larkin Shinnston, West Virginia

Cranberry Shortbread Bars

prep: 20 min. **bake:** 30 min. + cooling

1 cup butter, softened
1/2 cup confectioners' sugar
1 egg
1-1/2 cups all-purpose flour
1/2 cup flaked coconut
1/8 teaspoon salt
1/2 cup sugar
1/2 cup packed brown sugar
3 tablespoons cornstarch
1 package (12 ounces) fresh *or* frozen cranberries
1 cup unsweetened apple juice
1 cup chopped walnuts
2 squares (1 ounce *each*) white baking chocolate, melted

In a large mixing bowl, cream butter and confectioners' sugar. Beat in egg. Combine the flour, coconut and salt; gradually add to creamed mixture. Set aside 1 cup for topping. Spread remaining mixture into a greased 13-in. x 9-in. x 2-in. baking dish. Bake at 425° for 10 minutes.

Meanwhile, in a small saucepan, combine the sugars and cornstarch. Stir in cranberries and apple juice. Bring to a boil. Reduce heat; cook and stir for 5 minutes or until thickened. Remove from the heat; stir in walnuts.

Spread over crust. Sprinkle with reserved crumb mixture. Bake for 20-25 minutes or until golden brown and bubbly. Cool on a wire rack. Drizzle with white chocolate. Cut into bars. **Yield:** 2 dozen.

We combined nuts, cranberries, coconut and white chocolate to come up with these colorful and tasty bars. With a glass of milk, they make the perfect snack or dessert.
—*Taste of Home Test Kitchen*

Peanut Butter Crumb Apple Pie

prep: 10 min. **bake:** 20 min. + cooling

1 can (21 ounces) apple pie filling
1 teaspoon lemon juice
1 pastry shell (9 inches), baked
1/2 cup all-purpose flour
1/3 cup packed brown sugar
1 to 3 teaspoons grated lemon peel
1/2 teaspoon ground cinnamon
1/4 teaspoon ground nutmeg
6 tablespoons chunky peanut butter
2 tablespoons cold butter

Combine the pie filling and lemon juice; spoon into pastry shell. In a large bowl, combine flour, brown sugar, lemon peel, cinnamon and nutmeg; cut in peanut butter and butter until crumbly. Sprinkle over filling. Bake at 400° for 20-22 minutes or until topping is lightly browned. Cool on wire rack. **Yield:** 6-8 servings.

I use time-saving apple pie filling and a prepared pie crust for this scrumptious streusel-topped dessert.
—Billie Moss
Walnut Creek, California

(tip) **Crisp Crusts:** To prevent a soggy crust when baking Peanut Butter Crumb Apple Pie, wait until just before baking to place the pie filling in the pastry shell.

Cherry Almond Bars

prep: 10 min. **bake:** 40 min. + cooling

- 2 cups all-purpose flour
- 1/2 cup packed brown sugar
- 1 cup cold butter
- 1 cup golden raisins
- 1 cup chopped red *and/or* green maraschino cherries
- 1 cup sliced almonds
- 1 can (14 ounces) sweetened condensed milk

In a bowl, combine flour and brown sugar; cut in butter until crumbly. Press into an ungreased 15-in. x 10-in. x 1-in. baking pan. Bake at 325° for 12-14 minutes or until lightly browned.

Sprinkle with raisins, cherries and almonds; drizzle with milk. Bake 25-30 minutes longer or until golden brown. Cool on a wire rack. Cut into squares. **Yield:** 4 dozen.

A sweet lady I used to work for gave me this recipe. It's so easy, festive-looking and delicious.
—Ruth Ann Stelfox Raymond, Alberta

Shortcut Shortcake

prep: 20 min. + chilling

- 2 cups cold milk
- 1 package (5.1 ounces) instant vanilla pudding mix
- 1 package (15 ounces) cream-filled sponge cakes
- 4 cups sliced fresh strawberries
- 1 carton (8 ounces) frozen whipped topping, thawed

Additional strawberries, halved, optional

In a large bowl, whisk milk and pudding mix for 2 minutes. Let stand for 2 minutes or until soft-set; set aside. Slice sponge cakes in half lengthwise; place filling side up in an ungreased 13-in. x 9-in. x 2-in. dish. Spread pudding over the top.

Arrange sliced strawberries over pudding. Spread whipped topping over berries. Cover and refrigerate at least 1 hour before cutting. Garnish with strawberry halves if desired. Refrigerate leftovers. **Yield:** 12-15 servings.

Fresh strawberries, instant pudding and Twinkies make this shortcake fast and flavorful. —Jo Smith
Camden, Arkansas

⑩ Toffee Coffee Ice Cream

prep/total time: 10 min.

- 1 pint coffee ice cream, softened
- 1/4 cup miniature marshmallows
- 1/4 cup milk chocolate-covered almonds, halved
- 1 English toffee candy bar, chopped

In a bowl, combine the ice cream, marshmallows, almonds and chopped candy bar until blended. Serve immediately. **Yield:** 5 servings.

Need an afternoon pick-me-up? Try this grown-up blend of coffee ice cream with chocolaty almonds, toffee bits and mini marshmallows. It'll perk up your day. —Taste of Home Test Kitchen

Caramel Butter-Pecan Bars

prep: 10 min. **bake:** 15 min. + cooling

- 2 cups all-purpose flour
- 1 cup packed brown sugar
- 3/4 cup cold butter
- 1-1/2 cups chopped pecans
- 1 jar (12 ounces) caramel ice cream topping, warmed
- 1 package (11-1/2 ounces) milk chocolate chips

In a bowl, combine flour and brown sugar; cut in butter until crumbly. Press into an ungreased 13-in. x 9-in. x 2-in. baking dish. Top with pecans. Drizzle caramel topping evenly over pecans.

Bake at 350° for 15-20 minutes or until caramel is bubbly. Place on a wire rack. Sprinkle with chocolate chips. Let stand for 5 minutes. Carefully spread chips over caramel layer. Cool at room temperature for at least 6 hours or until chocolate is set. Cut into bars. **Yield:** 4 dozen.

These sweet, rich bars are to die for! Because the chocolate layer takes some time to harden, I like to fix these treats early in the day. —Mary Jean Hlavac
McFarland, Wisconsin

⑩ Cranberry Mallow Dessert

prep/total time: 5 min.

- 1 can (16 ounces) whole-berry cranberry sauce
- 2 cups miniature marshmallows
- 1 can (8 ounces) crushed pineapple, drained
- 1 teaspoon lemon juice
- 2 cups whipped topping

In a large bowl, combine the cranberry sauce, marshmallows, pineapple and lemon juice. Fold in whipped topping. Transfer to a serving dish. Cover and refrigerate until serving. **Yield:** 6-8 servings.

A holiday tradition at my house, this fluffy salad seems lighter than air. It's a great alternative to plain cranberry sauce and an easy potluck dish for seasonal get-togethers. It doubles as a refreshing dessert. —Cristie Hunt
Rossville, Georgia

Frozen Sandwich Cookies 30

prep/total time: 30 min.

1/2 cup spreadable strawberry cream
     cheese
1/4 cup strawberry yogurt
16   chocolate wafers

In a small mixing bowl, beat cream cheese and yogurt until smooth. Spread on the bottoms of half of the chocolate wafers; top with remaining wafers. Place on a baking sheet. Cover and freeze for 25 minutes. Serve or wrap in plastic wrap and store in the freezer.
Yield: 8 cookies.

These cool, creamy treats are a snap to make! Calling for just three ingredients, the cute, tasty cookies will be a hit with both young and old alike.
—Mary Ann Gómez
Lombard, Illinois

(tip) **More Frozen Treats:** Sandwich any cookies, brownies or graham crackers with your favorite flavor of ice cream. Try vanilla ice cream with oatmeal or chocolate chip cookies...fudge ripple or mint with brownies... strawberry with graham crackers.

Cinnamon Apple Crumb Pie

prep: 15 min. **bake:** 50 min. + cooling

- 1 can (21 ounces) apple pie filling
- 1 unbaked pastry shell (9 inches)
- 1/2 teaspoon ground cinnamon
- 4 tablespoons butter, *divided*
- 1-1/2 to 2 cups crushed pecan shortbread cookies

Pour pie filling into pastry shell. Sprinkle with cinnamon and dot with 1 tablespoon butter. Melt remaining butter. Place cookie crumbs in a small bowl; stir in butter until coarse crumbs form. Sprinkle over filling. Cover edges of pastry loosely with foil.

Bake at 450° for 10 minutes. Reduce heat to 350°; remove foil and bake for 40-45 minutes or until crust is golden brown and filling is bubbly. Cool on a wire rack for at least 2 hours. **Yield:** 6-8 servings.

Here's a dessert any busy hostess could love! It goes together in minutes, tastes like you fussed and is easily doubled to feed any size gathering.
—Carolyn Ruch
New London, Wisconsin

Blueberry Peach Cobbler

prep: 20 min. **bake:** 25 min.

1/2 **cup packed brown sugar**
3 **tablespoons cornstarch**
1/4 **teaspoon ground mace**
1/4 **cup sherry *or* unsweetened apple juice**
5 **cups sliced peeled peaches**
1 **cup fresh *or* frozen blueberries**
1/2 **cup chopped pecans**
1 **tablespoon butter**
1 **tablespoon lemon juice**
TOPPING:
1 **cup all-purpose flour**
1/3 **cup sugar**
1-1/2 **teaspoons baking powder**
Dash salt
1/4 **cup cold butter**
1/4 **cup milk**
1 **egg, lightly beaten**

In a large saucepan, combine the brown sugar, cornstarch and mace. Stir in sherry or juice until blended. Bring to a boil; cook and stir for 1-2 minutes or until thickened. Add the peaches, blueberries, pecans, butter and lemon juice. Pour into a greased shallow 2-qt. baking dish.

For topping, in a small bowl, combine the flour, sugar, baking powder and salt. Cut in butter until coarse crumbs form. Stir in milk and egg. Spoon over fruit mixture. Bake at 400° for 25-30 minutes or until bubbly and a toothpick inserted in the topping comes out clean. Serve warm. **Yield:** 6-8 servings.

This delicious cobbler smells so good while it's in the oven, your mouth will be watering before it's finished baking. Believe me—there will be no leftovers! —Roni Goodell Spanish Fork, Utah

Spice Substitution: If you don't have ground mace for the Blueberry Peach Cobbler, replace it with the same amount of nutmeg. Mace is the membrane that covers the nutmeg seed, so your dessert will have a similar flavor.

Cranberry Pecan Sandies

prep: 20 min. **bake:** 15 min. per batch

1 package (15.6 ounces) cranberry-orange quick bread mix
1/2 cup butter, melted
1 egg
2 tablespoons orange juice
3/4 cup chopped pecans
30 to 36 pecan halves
ORANGE GLAZE:
1 cup confectioners' sugar
3 to 4 teaspoons orange juice

In a large mixing bowl, combine the bread mix, butter, egg and orange juice. Stir in chopped pecans. Roll into 1-in. balls. Place 2 in. apart on ungreased baking sheets. Flatten with the bottom of a glass coated with non-stick cooking spray. Press a pecan half into center of each cookie.

Bake at 350° for 12-14 minutes or until lightly browned. Cool for 1 minute before removing to wire racks. In a small bowl, whisk glaze ingredients. Drizzle over cookies. **Yield:** 2-1/2 to 3 dozen.

These delicate, crisp cookies are flavored with pecans, cranberry and a hint of orange.
—Teresa Jarrell
Danville, West Virginia

Storing Cookies: (tip)
Allow cookies to cool completely and icing to completely dry before storing. Layer in a container, separating each layer with waxed paper.

Apple Snack Cake

prep: 15 min. **bake:** 35 min. + cooling

1/2 cup butter, softened
1/2 cup packed brown sugar
3 eggs
1 teaspoon vanilla extract
1 package (15.4 ounces) nut quick bread mix
1 teaspoon ground cinnamon
2 medium tart apples, peeled and finely chopped
1/2 cup raisins
ICING:
3/4 cup confectioners' sugar
1/4 teaspoon ground cinnamon
2 tablespoons butter, melted
1/4 teaspoon vanilla extract
3 to 5 tablespoons milk

In a large mixing bowl, cream the butter and brown sugar. Beat in eggs and vanilla. Add quick bread mix and cinnamon; beat until combined. Fold in apples and raisins. Transfer to a greased 13-in. x 9-in. x 2-in. baking dish. Bake at 350° for 35-40 minutes or until a toothpick inserted near the center comes out clean. Cool on a wire rack.

In a small bowl, combine the confectioners' sugar, cinnamon, butter, vanilla and enough milk to achieve desired consistency. Drizzle over cake. **Yield:** 12-15 servings.

A package of quick bread mix is the secret behind this speedy spice cake. Moist and flecked with bits of apple, it's excellent for dessert or as a breakfast treat with a cup of coffee.
—Marilyn Terman
Columbus, Ohio

Light Strawberry Pie

prep: 25 min. + chilling

- 1 can (8 ounces) unsweetened crushed pineapple
- 1 package (.8 ounce) sugar-free cook-and-serve vanilla pudding mix
- 1 package (.3 ounce) sugar-free strawberry gelatin
- 3 cups sliced fresh strawberries
- 1 reduced-fat graham cracker crust (8 inches)
- 1/2 cup reduced-fat whipped topping

Drain pineapple, reserving juice in a 2-cup measuring cup. Set pineapple aside. Add enough water to juice to measure 1-1/2 cups; transfer to a saucepan. Whisk in the pudding mix and gelatin until combined. Bring to a boil; cook and stir for 1-2 minutes or until thickened. Stir in pineapple. Remove from the heat; cool for 10 minutes.

Add the strawberries; toss gently to coat. Pour into crust. Refrigerate until set, about 3 hours. Garnish each piece with 1 tablespoon whipped topping. Refrigerate any leftovers. **Yield:** 8 servings.

This berry dessert offers luscious taste and make-ahead convenience. People rave about this pie. Best of all, it's a low-sugar treat that you won't feel one bit guilty eating.
—Lou Wright
Rockford, Illinois

Berry Good Alternative: **tip**
Fresh raspberries and raspberry gelatin can be used in place of the strawberries with equally delicious results.

Pineapple Crunch

prep: 15 min. **bake:** 10 min. + cooling

1 cup crushed cornflakes
2 tablespoons sugar
1/3 cup butter, melted
2 tablespoons cornstarch
2 cans (8 ounces *each*) crushed pineapple, undrained
2 cups vanilla ice cream, softened
1 package (3.4 ounces) instant vanilla pudding mix

In a bowl, combine the cornflake crumbs, sugar and butter. Press into a greased 9-in. square baking dish. Bake at 350° for 10 minutes. Cool on a wire rack.

In a saucepan, combine the cornstarch and pineapple until blended. Bring to a boil; cook and stir for 2 minutes or until thickened. Cool. In a mixing bowl, beat the ice cream and pudding mix on low speed for 2 minutes or until blended and thickened. Spoon over crust. Top with pineapple mixture. Refrigerate until serving. **Yield:** 9-12 servings.

My crunchy pineapple dessert offers quick refreshment. This recipe was given to me years ago by a co-worker. Every time I take it somewhere, it's a favorite. —Betty Wiersma Sherwood Park, Alberta

Coconut Ice Cream Torte

prep: 15 min. + freezing

18 macaroons, crushed
1/4 cup butter, melted
3/4 cup hot fudge ice cream topping
26 snack-size Mounds *or* Almond Joy candy bars
1 quart vanilla ice cream, softened
1 quart strawberry ice cream, softened
1/4 cup sliced almonds, toasted

In a small bowl, combine cookie crumbs and butter. Press onto the bottom of a greased 10-in. springform pan. Freeze for 15 minutes.

In a microwave-safe bowl, heat hot fudge topping on high for 15-20 seconds or until pourable; spread over crust. Arrange candy bars around the edge of pan. Freeze for 15 minutes. Spread vanilla ice cream over fudge topping; freeze for 30 minutes.

Spread strawberry ice cream over vanilla layer; sprinkle with almonds. Cover and freeze until firm. May be frozen for up to 2 months. Remove from the freezer 10 minutes before serving. Remove sides of the pan. **Yield:** 13 servings.

Editor's Note: If Almond Joy candy bars are used, arrange bars with almond side facing inward toward the center of the pan.

Guests will ooh and aah when you bring out this fabulous ice cream torte ringed with snack-size Mounds bars. But this is one showstopper definitely created with busy hostesses in mind. It's super easy, feeds a crowd and can be made days ahead for convenience.
—*Taste of Home Test Kitchen*

Caramel Peanut Fantasy

prep: 30 min. + chilling

2 cups vanilla wafer crumbs
1/3 cup butter, melted
20 caramels
15 miniature Snickers candy bars
1/2 cup caramel ice cream topping
1/2 cup heavy whipping cream, *divided*
2 cups salted peanuts, chopped
3/4 cup semisweet chocolate chips

In a small bowl, combine wafer crumbs and butter. Press onto the bottom of a greased 9-in. springform pan. Place on a baking sheet. Bake at 350° for 8-10 minutes. Cool on a wire rack.

In a heavy saucepan, combine caramels, candy bars, caramel topping and 1/4 cup cream; cook and stir over low heat until smooth and blended. Remove from the heat; stir in peanuts. Spread over crust. Cover and refrigerate for 1 hour.

In a saucepan or microwave, melt chocolate chips and remaining cream. Spread over caramel layer. Cover and refrigerate for 1 hour or until serving. **Yield:** 12 servings.

Packed with peanuts and gooey with caramel, this do-ahead treat is one sweet dream of a dessert to serve company. With an easy cookie crust and scrumptious layers, it goes together in a snap...and will disappear just as fast!
—Taste of Home Test Kitchen

Simple Swap: Try different ice cream toppings or candy bars in either of these recipes to vary the flavor to suit your taste.

20 Cookie Pizza a la Mode

prep/total time: 20 min.

1 tube (18 ounces) refrigerated
chocolate chip cookie dough
Chocolate syrup
Vanilla ice cream
6 maraschino cherries, optional

Press the cookie dough onto an ungreased 12-in. pizza pan. Bake at 400° for 12-14 minutes or until golden brown. Cool on a wire rack for 5 minutes. Cut into six wedges.

Drizzle chocolate syrup over dessert plates. Top with warm cookie wedges, ice cream and additional chocolate syrup. Garnish each wedge with a cherry if desired. **Yield:** 6 servings.

This is my rendition of a dessert we enjoyed at a restaurant. People always tell me it's delicious.
—Dee Drew
Aliso Viejo, California

Chocolate Peanut Grahams

prep: 10 min. + chilling

4 cinnamon graham crackers,
    broken into quarters
1/4 cup creamy peanut butter
1 cup (6 ounces) semisweet
    chocolate chips
3 teaspoons shortening

Spread half of the graham cracker quarters with peanut butter; top with remaining crackers. In a microwave-safe bowl, melt chocolate chips and shortening; stir until smooth. Dip the crackers into chocolate; place on a waxed paper-lined pan. Refrigerate until set. **Yield:** 8 treats.

Convenient cinnamon graham crackers are the base for these tasty chocolaty treats.
—Taste of Home Test Kitchen

(tip) Easy Assembly: Children will get a kick out of making these chocolate-peanut butter treats. Get the ingredients together and have the kids assemble them while you're preparing dinner. Consider making a double or triple batch, then freeze some for a fast snack from the freezer.

Caramel Chocolate Cake

prep: 25 min. + cooling **bake:** 30 min. + cooling

3/4 cup packed brown sugar
6 tablespoons butter, cubed
2 tablespoons plus 1 cup cold milk, *divided*
1/2 cup chopped pecans
1 package (18-1/4 ounces) German chocolate cake mix
1 package (3.4 ounces) instant butterscotch pudding mix
2 cups whipped topping

In a small saucepan, combine the brown sugar, butter and 2 tablespoons milk. Cook and stir over low heat until sugar is dissolved. Increase heat to medium. Do not stir. Cook for 3-6 minutes or until bubbles form in center of mixture and color is amber brown. Remove from the heat; stir in pecans. Cool to room temperature, stirring occasionally.

Meanwhile, prepare and bake cake according to package directions for two 9-in. round baking pans. Cool for 10 minutes before removing from pans to wire racks to cool completely.

In a bowl, whisk pudding mix and remaining milk until smooth. Fold in whipped topping. Cover and refrigerate until thickened, about 20 minutes.

Place one cake layer on a serving platter; spread with 3/4 cup pudding mixture. Top with remaining cake layer; spread remaining pudding mixture over top and sides of cake. Spoon pecan mixture around top edge. Store in the refrigerator. **Yield:** 10-12 servings.

Chocolate cake from a boxed mix gets a special treatment when spread with an easy butterscotch frosting and accented with a caramel-nut topping. I love to make this cake for guests or to take to potlucks. It's easy yet looks like it took all day.
—Gloria Guadron
Washington, Indiana

Topped Cheesecake Squares

prep: 30 min. **bake:** 30 min. + chilling

1-1/4 cups chocolate wafer crumbs
1/4 cup butter, melted
2 packages (8 ounces *each*) cream cheese, softened
2/3 cup plus 2 tablespoons sugar, *divided*
2 eggs, lightly beaten
1-1/2 teaspoons vanilla extract, *divided*
1/4 teaspoon almond extract
1 cup (8 ounces) sour cream

CHOCOLATE STRAWBERRIES:
2 ounces dark chocolate candy bar
3 fresh strawberries
1 square (1 ounce) white baking chocolate

CARAMEL TOPPING:
6 caramels
1 tablespoon heavy whipping cream
Whipped cream
1 tablespoon sliced almonds, toasted

BERRY TOPPING:
1/4 cup seedless raspberry jam
6 fresh raspberries
6 fresh blackberries
6 fresh blueberries

In a bowl, combine crumbs and butter. Press firmly onto bottom of an 8-in. square baking dish. In a small mixing bowl, beat cream cheese and 2/3 cup sugar until smooth. Add eggs; beat on low speed just until combined. Stir in 1/2 teaspoon vanilla and almond extract. Pour over crust. Bake at 325° for 25 minutes or until set. Cool for 5 minutes.

Meanwhile, in a small bowl, combine the sour cream and the remaining sugar and vanilla. Spread over filling; bake 5 minutes longer. Cool on a wire rack for 1 hour. Refrigerate for at least 5 hours or overnight.

In a small microwave-safe bowl, melt candy bar at 50% power; stir until smooth. Dip bottoms of strawberries in chocolate and place on a waxed paper-lined baking sheet to set. Microwave white chocolate, uncovered, at 50% power until melted; stir until smooth. Drizzle over the strawberries. Refrigerate until serving. Just before serving, cut cheesecake into nine squares. Place chocolate strawberries on three squares.

For caramel topping, in a small microwave-safe bowl, combine caramels and cream. Microwave, uncovered, on high for 45 seconds, stirring once. Spoon over three cheesecake squares. Top with a dollop of whipped cream. Sprinkle with almonds.

For berry topping, in a small microwave-safe bowl, combine jam and berries. Microwave, uncovered, on high for 45 seconds, stirring once. Spoon over remaining squares. **Yield:** 9 servings.

Editor's Note: This recipe was tested in a 1,100-watt microwave.

These rich cheesecake squares can be dressed up three ways. Let family and friends choose from a chocolate-dipped strawberry, a warm drizzle of caramel and almonds, or a dollop of fresh fruit and jam.
—Taste of Home Test Kitchen

Strawberry Apple Pie

prep: 15 min. **bake:** 45 min.

3-1/2 cups thinly sliced peeled Granny
       Smith apples (about 3 medium)
1-1/4 cups sliced fresh strawberries
   1 tablespoon lemon juice
 1/2 cup sugar
   3 to 4 tablespoons all-purpose flour
Pastry for double-crust pie (9 inches)
TOPPING:
 1/2 teaspoon sugar
 1/8 teaspoon ground cinnamon
Whipped topping, optional

In a large bowl, combine the apples and strawberries; drizzle with the lemon juice. Combine sugar and flour; sprinkle over fruit and toss lightly.

Line a 9-in. pie plate with bottom pastry; trim even with edge of plate. Add filling. Roll out remaining pastry to fit top of pie; place over filling. Trim, seal and flute edges. Cut slits in top. Combine sugar and cinnamon; sprinkle over pastry. Cover edges loosely with foil.

Bake at 450° for 10 minutes. Reduce heat to 350°; remove foil and bake 35-40 minutes longer or until crust is golden brown and filling is bubbly. Cool on a wire rack. Garnish with whipped topping if desired. **Yield:** 6-8 servings.

I ran short of apples when baking an apple pie to bring to dinner at my in-laws. I substituted strawberries for the rest of the apples and didn't tell anyone. But that pie was such a hit, I've been making it ever since!
—Dianne Ebke
Plymouth, Nebraska

Chocolate Mousse Torte

prep: 15 min. + chilling

2 packages (3 ounces *each*) ladyfingers, split
2 cups cold milk
3 packages (2.8 ounces *each*) chocolate mousse mix
3 cups whipped topping, *divided*
Fresh raspberries

Line the bottom and sides of a lightly greased 9-in. springform pan with ladyfingers (save remaining ladyfingers for another use).

In a large mixing bowl, beat milk and mousse mixes on medium speed for 1 minute; scrape sides of bowl. Beat on high for 2-3 minutes or until thickened and lighter in color. Remove half of the mousse to another bowl; fold in 1/2 cup whipped topping. Spread over crust.

Fold remaining whipped topping into remaining mousse; carefully spread over first layer. Refrigerate for 4 hours or overnight. Garnish with raspberries. **Yield:** 12 servings.

Editor's Note: This recipe was tested with Nestlé European Style Mousse Mix.

This lovely, make-ahead dessert needs just a few minutes and a few ingredients. Rich, creamy mousse layers are surrounded by ladyfingers and topped with fresh berries for a gorgeous garnish.
—Taste of Home Test Kitchen

(tip) **Leftover Ladyfingers:** Make easy, elegant parfaits in minutes. Crumble a couple ladyfingers in each parfait glass, drizzle with orange liqueur, top with fresh berries and dollop with whipped cream.

⏱10 Sorbet Cream Puffs

prep/total time: 10 min.

1 cup mixed fresh berries
1 tablespoon sugar
2 cups peach sorbet
4 cream puff shells
Whipped cream

In a small bowl, combine berries and sugar. Place a scoop of sorbet in each cream puff shell; dollop with whipped cream. Replace tops and serve with the berry mixture. **Yield:** 4 servings.

Simple and pretty as a picture, these dainty, refreshing treats will melt any resistance to dessert! Best of all, they couldn't be easier to make. Garnish with fresh berries or whatever fruit you prefer.
—Taste of Home Test Kitchen

Puff Pastry Pointer: **(tip)**
Make a batch of plain cream puffs and keep them on hand in your freezer to make these pretty treats. Or use phyllo shells, found in the freezer section of your grocery store.

Pistachio Eclair Dessert

prep: 20 min. + chilling

3 cups cold milk
1 package (3.4 ounces) instant pistachio pudding mix
1 package (3.4 ounces) instant French vanilla pudding mix
1 carton (8 ounces) frozen whipped topping, thawed
1 package (14.4 ounces) graham crackers
1 can (16 ounces) chocolate frosting

In a large bowl, whisk milk and pudding mixes for 2 minutes. Let stand for 2 minutes or until soft-set. Fold in whipped topping. In a 13-in. x 9-in. x 2-in. dish, layer a third of the graham crackers and half of the pudding mixture. Repeat layers. Top with remaining graham crackers. Refrigerate for at least 1 hour.

Spoon the frosting into a microwave-safe bowl. Cover and microwave on high for 15-20 seconds or until softened, stirring once. Spread over graham crackers. Chill for at least 20 minutes or until frosting is set. **Yield:** 15-20 servings.

This yummy dessert whips up in minutes and can be chilled until ready to serve. It's tasty and easy to fix. I've often brought it to family gatherings and office parties, and it's always the first to go.
—Lisa Givens
Austin, Texas

Zucchini Brownies

prep: 20 min. **bake:** 35 min. + cooling

1 cup butter, softened
1-1/2 cups sugar
2 eggs
1/2 cup plain yogurt
1 teaspoon vanilla extract
2-1/2 cups all-purpose flour
1/4 cup baking cocoa
1 teaspoon baking soda
1/2 teaspoon salt
2 cups shredded zucchini
FROSTING:
2/3 cup semisweet chocolate chips
1/2 cup creamy peanut butter

In a large mixing bowl, cream butter and sugar. Add eggs, one at a time, beating well after each addition. Beat in yogurt and vanilla. Combine the flour, cocoa, baking soda and salt; gradually add to creamed mixture. Fold in zucchini.

Pour into a greased 13-in. x 9-in. x 2-in. baking pan. Bake at 350° for 35-40 minutes or until a toothpick inserted near the center comes out clean.

For frosting, combine chocolate chips and peanut butter in a small saucepan. Cook and stir over low heat until smooth. Spread over warm brownies. Cool on a wire rack. Cut into bars. **Yield:** about 1-1/2 dozen.

A fast-to-fix peanut butter and chocolate frosting tops these moist brownies that are a sweet way to use up your green garden squash. We really like the cake-like texture of these brownies.
—Allyson Wilkins
Amherst, New Hampshire

Layered Lemon Pie (30)

prep/total time: 25 min.

1 package (8 ounces) cream cheese, softened
1/2 cup sugar
1 can (15-3/4 ounces) lemon pie filling
1 carton (8 ounces) frozen whipped topping, thawed
1 graham cracker crust (9 inches)

In a small mixing bowl, beat the cream cheese and sugar until smooth. Beat in half of the pie filling. Fold in the whipped topping. Spoon into crust. Spread with remaining pie filling. Refrigerate for 15 minutes or until serving. Refrigerate leftovers. **Yield:** 8 servings.

This is a great ending for almost any meal...and one that both kids and adults will enjoy. The creamy lemon filling is always a hit with my husband.
—Elizabeth Yoder
Belcourt, North Dakota

(tip) **Pie Keeper:** Not sure if your pie needs to be refrigerated? Pies made with eggs, milk, sour cream, whipped cream, whipped topping, yogurt or cream cheese should be refrigerated as soon as possible after they're prepared. Baked pies made with any of these ingredients should cool for about an hour before being refrigerated.

(30) French Vanilla Bread Pudding

prep/total time: 25 min.

2 slices cinnamon-raisin bread, cubed
1 egg
1/2 cup refrigerated French vanilla nondairy creamer
1 caramel, cut into small pieces
1 tablespoon chopped pecans
1/4 teaspoon ground cinnamon
1 tablespoon butter

Place the bread cubes in two greased 6-oz. ramekins or custard cups. In a small bowl, whisk egg and creamer; pour over bread. Sprinkle with caramel pieces, pecans and cinnamon; dot with butter. Bake at 350° for 18-20 minutes or until bubbly and golden brown. Cool slightly before serving. **Yield:** 2 servings.

For a comforting ending to a meal, dig into this bread pudding. With caramel, pecans and cinnamon, each bite is simply irresistible.
—Nancy Johnson
Laverne, Oklahoma

Make It for a Larger Family: (tip) This recipe is simple to double or triple to feed a larger family. You can also vary the flavor of nondairy creamer; try amaretto, creme brulee, hazelnut or vanilla caramel.

Family-Favorite Poke Cake

prep: 10 min. **bake:** 35 min. + cooling

- 1 package (18-1/4 ounces) yellow cake mix
- 10 fun-size Milky Way candy bars, *divided*
- 1 can (14 ounces) sweetened condensed milk
- 1 jar (12 ounces) Milky Way ice cream topping
- 1 carton (12 ounces) frozen whipped topping, thawed

Prepare and bake cake according to package directions, using a greased 13-in. x 9-in. x 2-in. baking pan. Chop six candy bars. Remove cake from the oven; immediately sprinkle with chopped candy bars. Cool on a wire rack for 10 minutes.

Using the end of a wooden spoon handle, poke 20 holes in warm cake. Pour milk over cake; cool for 10 minutes. Pour the ice cream topping over cake; cool completely. Spread whipped topping over cake. Chop remaining candy bars; sprinkle over cake. Cover and store in the refrigerator. **Yield:** 12-15 servings.

I need only a handful of ingredients for my yummy version of popular poke cake. It's so simple, kids may want to whip it up themselves! —Kristine Sims
St. Joseph, Michigan

30 Snickerdoodle Sundaes

prep/total time: 30 min.

- 1 package (17-1/2 ounces) sugar cookie mix
- 2 cups cinnamon ice cream *or* ice cream of your choice
- 1/2 cup caramel ice cream topping

Prepare and bake the cookies according to package directions. Set aside 8 cookies (save remaining cookies for another use). Place 2 cookies in each serving bowl. Top with 1/2 cup ice cream; drizzle with 2 tablespoons caramel topping. **Yield:** 4 servings.

I was baking sugar cookies with my two daughters when a friend brought over some cinnamon ice cream. The two items were a perfect match!
—Melissa Van Bramer, Pickerington, Ohio

Raspberry Coconut Cake

prep: 20 min. **bake:** 25 min. + cooling

- 1 package (18-1/4 ounces) white cake mix
- 3 cups flaked coconut, *divided*
- 6 squares (1 ounce *each*) white baking chocolate
- 1/4 cup heavy whipping cream
- 3/4 cup seedless raspberry jam
- 1 cup butter, softened
- 1 cup confectioners' sugar

Prepare cake batter according to package directions; fold in 2/3 cup coconut. Pour into two greased 9-in. round baking pans. Bake at 350° for 25-30 minutes or until a toothpick inserted near the center comes out clean. Cool for 10 minutes before removing from pans to wire racks to cool completely.

In a microwave-safe bowl, combine white chocolate and cream. Microwave, uncovered, on high for 1 minute or until chocolate is almost melted; stir until smooth. Cool to room temperature. In a small bowl, combine jam and 1 cup coconut. Spread over one cake layer; top with second layer.

In a small mixing bowl, cream butter and confectioners' sugar until light and fluffy; gradually beat in white chocolate mixture. Spread over top and sides of cake. Toast remaining coconut; sprinkle over cake. **Yield:** 12 servings.

Editor's Note: This recipe was tested in a 1,100-watt microwave.

This looked like a pretty dessert to make for the holidays, so I decided to try it out on my co-workers. They loved it!
—Joanie Ward
Brownsburg, Indiana

Timely Toasting: **(tip)**

It's easy to toast coconut for Raspberry Coconut Cake. To toast it in the oven, place in a shallow baking pan and bake at 350°, stirring frequently, about 5 minutes or until golden brown. To toast it in the microwave, place it in a glass pie plate and microwave on high for 3 to 4 minutes, stirring every minute.

Chocolate Almond Fondue

prep/total time: 20 min.

- 3/4 cup heavy whipping cream
- 2 milk chocolate candy bars (5 ounces *each*), chopped
- 1 jar (7 ounces) marshmallow creme
- 3 squares (1 ounce *each*) white baking chocolate, chopped
- 1/4 cup chopped almonds, toasted
- 3 tablespoons amaretto *or* 1/2 teaspoon almond extract

Assorted fresh fruit and pound cake cubes

In a heavy saucepan, heat cream over low heat until warmed. Add the candy bars, marshmallow creme and white chocolate; stir until melted. Stir in the almonds and amaretto or almond extract. Transfer to a fondue pot and keep warm. Serve with fruit and cake cubes. **Yield:** about 4 cups.

This is a luscious dip for fresh fruit and cake cubes. Since fondue has become popular again, I've had fun searching out recipes that are fast and especially delicious. This one's a favorite. —Angela Hutton
Kapolei, Hawaii

Mint Chip Deluxe

prep/total time: 10 min.

- 1 pint mint chocolate chip ice cream, softened
- 1 prepared brownie, chopped
- 6 mint Andes candies, chopped

In a bowl, combine the ice cream, brownie and chopped candies. Serve immediately. **Yield:** 4 servings.

You'll need just three ingredients for this dressed-up treat. The brownie and candies make the mint ice cream taste decadent, but it comes together in a dash. —Taste of Home Test Kitchen

20 Sparkling Fresh Fruit

prep/total time: 15 min.

- 1-1/2 cups sliced fresh strawberries
- 1-1/2 cups fresh blueberries
- 1 cup cubed cantaloupe
- 4 scoops raspberry sherbet *or* flavor of your choice
- 1 cup champagne *or* lemon-lime soda

Combine strawberries, blueberries and cantaloupe; divide among four dessert dishes. Top each with a scoop of sherbet. Drizzle with champagne or soda. Serve immediately. **Yield:** 4 servings.

Individual dishes of this fruit make a pretty finale to any meal. You can prepare it with cut-up fruit from the produce department if you're short on time. For an elegant touch, I garnish it with fresh mint sprigs. —Nancee Melin, Tucson, Arizona

desserts

⑳ Angel Peach Melba

prep/total time: 15 min.

1 package (12 ounces) frozen
   unsweetened raspberries, thawed
2 tablespoons sugar
1 loaf (8 ounces) angel food cake,
   cut into 10 slices
1 can (16 ounces) peach halves,
   drained
2-1/2 cups vanilla frozen yogurt

In a small bowl, combine the raspberries and sugar; set aside. Place cake slices on an ungreased baking sheet. Broil 4 in. from the heat for 1-2 minutes on each side or until lightly toasted. Using a 2-1/2-in. biscuit cutter, cut a hole in the center of each slice. Remove cutouts and set aside.

Place each cake slice in an individual bowl; place a peach half, cut side up, in each hole. Top each with a scoop of frozen yogurt and a reserved cake cutout. Drizzle with raspberry mixture. Serve immediately. **Yield:** 10 servings.

Store-bought angel food cake, canned peaches, frozen yogurt and raspberries combine to make a sweet, summery dessert in just minutes.
—Janice Prytz
Murrieta, California

- - - - - - - - - - - - - - - -

Vary the Berries: (tip)
Change up this melba recipe by using other berries and frozen yogurt flavors to suit your taste.

Poppy Seed Lemon Pie ⑩

prep/total time: 10 min.

1 can (14 ounces) sweetened
condensed milk
1/3 cup lemonade concentrate
1 carton (8 ounces) frozen whipped
topping, thawed, *divided*
1 graham cracker crust (9 inches)
1 tablespoon poppy seeds
10 to 12 drops yellow food coloring,
optional

In a mixing bowl, beat milk and lemonade concentrate until smooth (mixture will begin to thicken). Fold in 2 cups whipped topping. Spread half into the crust.

Add poppy seeds and food coloring, if desired, to the remaining lemon mixture; stir until blended. Spoon over first layer. Spread with the remaining whipped topping and refrigerate until serving. **Yield:** 6-8 servings.

Your family will love this tangy finale to dinner...and never guess how simple it is to prepare!
—*Taste of Home Test Kitchen*

⓴ Fresh Fruit Tartlets

prep/total time: 20 min.

1 envelope whipped topping mix
1/2 cup cold milk
1 teaspoon vanilla extract
1 package (8 ounces) cream cheese, softened
1/2 cup confectioners' sugar
10 individual graham cracker tart shells
Assorted fresh fruit

In a small mixing bowl, beat the topping mix, milk and vanilla on low speed until blended. Beat on high until soft peaks form, about 4 minutes. In a large mixing bowl, beat cream cheese and confectioners' sugar until smooth. Fold in the whipped topping mixture. Spoon into tart shells; top with fruit. Refrigerate leftovers. **Yield:** 10 servings.

These mini tarts are perfect for showers, parties or whenever you need a pretty dessert.
—Shelly Forslund
Delafield, Wisconsin

- - - - - - - - - - - - - - - -

Tasty Toppers: Top them with blueberries, mandarin orange segments, or sliced strawberries, kiwifruit, bananas or pineapple.

(tip)

Fudge-Filled Brownie Bars

prep: 10 min. **bake:** 30 min. + cooling

1-1/2 cups all-purpose flour
  3/4 cup packed brown sugar
  3/4 cup butter, softened
    1 egg yolk
  3/4 teaspoon vanilla extract
FILLING:
    1 package fudge brownie mix
      (13-inch x 9-inch pan size)
    1 egg
  1/3 cup water
  1/3 cup vegetable oil
TOPPING:
    1 package (11-1/2 ounces) milk
      chocolate chips, melted
  3/4 cup chopped walnuts, toasted

In a large bowl, combine the first five ingredients. Press onto the bottom of a greased 15-in. x 10-in. x 1-in. baking pan. Bake at 350° for 15-18 minutes or until golden brown.

Meanwhile, in a large bowl, combine the filling ingredients. Spread over hot crust. Bake for 15 minutes or until set. Cool on a wire rack for 30 minutes. Spread melted chocolate over filling; sprinkle with walnuts. Cool completely. Cut into bars. **Yield:** 4 dozen.

I always have the ingredients to put together these soft, chewy bars. They have been a hit at many potlucks. —Nola Burski, Lakeville, Minnesota

30 Strawberry Breadstick Rolls

prep/total time: 30 min.

  2 cups sliced fresh strawberries
  5 teaspoons sugar, *divided*
  1 tube (11 ounces) refrigerated breadsticks
  2 tablespoons butter, melted
  2 tablespoons brown sugar
  2 tablespoons maple syrup

In a small bowl, combine the strawberries and 2 teaspoons sugar; set aside. On a lightly floured surface, unroll breadstick dough (do not separate). Seal perforations; brush dough with butter. Combine brown sugar and remaining sugar; sprinkle over dough. Reroll, starting with a short end. Cut along seam lines.

Place rolls cut side down on a greased baking sheet. Bake at 375° for 11-13 minutes or until golden brown. Brush with syrup. Serve with reserved strawberry mixture. **Yield:** 6 servings.

For a simple dessert, bake these sweet, fruit-topped rolls that call for just six ingredients. They're so yummy, your family may request them for breakfast, too. —Taste of Home Test Kitchen

General Index

Strawberry Apple Pie, pg. 224

Fabulous Feta Salad, pg. 173

general index

CHICKEN

Apricot Chicken, 15

Barbecue Jack Chicken, 63

Cantonese Chicken Burgers, 145

Carrot Chicken Pilaf, 38

Chicken Breast Cacciatore, 36

Chicken Coleslaw Wraps, 54

Chicken Minestrone, 68

Chicken Pizza, 46

Chicken Satay Wraps, 24

Chicken Shepherd's Pie, 76

Chicken-Stuffed Tomatoes, 149

Chicken Wellington, 52

Chicken with Mustard Gravy, 77

Curry Chicken Salad Wraps, 135

Fruity Chicken Tossed Salad, 159

Garlic Chicken 'n' Gravy, 9

Guacamole Chicken Wraps, 118

Nacho Chicken Pitas, 48

Parmesan Chicken Pasta, 65

Quicker Chicken 'n' Dumplings, 30

Tortilla Soup, 119

Tossed Chicken Salad, 169

Almond Chip Scones, pg. 93

CHOCOLATE

Almond Chip Scones, 93

Banana Chocolate Parfaits, 202

Caramel Chocolate Cake, 222

Chocolate Almond Fondue, 233

Chocolate Chip Pancakes, 94

Chocolate Cranberry Cheesecake, 201

Chocolate Croissants, 98

Chocolate Mousse Torte, 225

Chocolate Peanut Grahams, 221

Fudge-Filled Brownie Bars, 237

Warm Chocolate Eggnog, 85

Zucchini Brownies, 228

COCONUT

Almond Coconut Bars, 203

Coconut Almond Muffins, 85

Coconut Ice Cream Torte, 218

Raspberry Coconut Cake, 232

COFFEE CAKE & PASTRIES

Caramel Sweet Rolls, 104

Chocolate Croissants, 98

Cinnamon Almond Braid, 82

Cran-Apple Cups, 83

Morning Cinnamon Rolls, 112

Strawberry Breadstick Rolls, 237

COOKIES & BARS

Almond Coconut Bars, 203

Candy Cookie Cups, 198

Caramel Butter-Pecan Bars, 209

Cherry Almond Bars, 208

Chocolate Peanut Grahams, 221

Cookie Pizza a la Mode, 220

Cranberry Pecan Sandies, 214

Cranberry Shortbread Bars, 206

Frozen Sandwich Cookies, 211

Fudge-Filled Brownie Bars, 237

Salty Peanut Squares, 196

Topped Cheesecake Squares, 223

Zucchini Brownies, 228

Blackened Fish Salad, pg. 59

general index

Salsa Pasta 'n' Beans, pg. 170

general index

Deep-Fried Cherry Pies, pg. 205

Special Sandwich Loaves, pg. 117

general index

Onion Soup with Sausage, pg. 122

Alphabetical Index

Barbecue Jack Chicken, pg. 63

Dressed-Up Steaks, pg. 47

alphabetical index

Fish Po'Boys, 41

Flank Steak with Couscous, 58

French Toast Supreme, 109

French Vanilla Bread Pudding, 230

Fresh Fruit Tartlets, 236

Fried Ice Cream, 199

Frozen Sandwich Cookies, 211

Fruit Slush, 102

Fruit Smoothies, 97

Fruity Baked Oatmeal, 105

Fruity Chicken Tossed Salad, 159

Fruity Peanut Butter Pitas, 107

Fudge-Filled Brownie Bars, 237

G

Garlic Chicken 'n' Gravy, 9

Garlic Oregano Zucchini, 176

Fruit Smoothies, pg. 97

Ginger-Apple Pork Chops, 10

Gingered Pepper Steak, 35

Grilled Ham 'n' Jack Cheese, 136

Grilled Rib Eyes, 12

Grilled Sourdough Clubs, 114

Guacamole Chicken Wraps, 118

H

Ham and Mango Wraps, 119

Hash Brown Apple Pancake, 183

Homemade Maple Syrup, 100

Honey Fruit Salad, 91

Hot Turkey Sandwiches, 119

I

Italian Veggie Skillet, 179

J

Jazzed-Up French Toast Sticks, 95

L

Layered Lemon Pie, 229

Layered Salad Reuben-Style, 182

Lemon-Linguine Shrimp Salad, 190

Lemon-Pepper Vegetables, 160

Lemon Strawberry Tarts, 204

Light 'n' Crispy Waffles, 100

Light Strawberry Pie, 216

Linguine with Garlic Sauce, 70

M

Microwave Potato Salad, 165

Mint Chip Deluxe, 233

Morning Cinnamon Rolls, 112

Mushroom Rice, 151

N

Nacho Chicken Pitas, 48

Parmesan Chicken Pasta, pg. 65

alphabetical index

Tuna Cheese Sandwiches, pg. 123

Recipe Time Index

10 MINUTE RECIPES

20 MINUTE RECIPES

Toffee-Flavored Coffee, pg. 95

recite time index

Beef Tips on Potatoes, pg. 51

Frozen Sandwich Cookies, pg. 211

recipe time index

Refried Bean Soup, pg. 121